generation
to
generation

Wayne Rice is one of the most influential leaders in the Christian family and youth ministry world. Generation to Generation *provides one of the most important messages to parents and church leaders for this decade. He gives us a biblical philosophy of parenting that will help us lead our families toward deeper faith.*

— Jim Burns, author of *Confident Parenting;*
founder and president, HomeWord

Wayne has written a wonderful book that will be a great encouragement to parents who want to lead their children to a strong and lasting faith in Christ.

— Dr. David Jeremiah, senior pastor,
Shadow Mountain Community Church;
founder and CEO, Turning Point

Practical and Creative Ideas for Raising Kids
to Know and Love God

generation
to
generation

WAYNE RICE

Standard®
PUBLISHING
Bringing The Word to Life

Cincinnati, Ohio

Published by Standard Publishing, Cincinnati, Ohio

www.standardpub.com

Printed in the United States of America

Editor: Robert Irvin
Cover design: Susan Koski Zucker
Interior design: Dina Sorn at Ahaa! Design

Cover photograph: Cristina McEwen

ISBN 978-0-7847-2125-4

Library of Congress Cataloging-in-Publication Data

Rice, Wayne.
  Generation to generation : practical and creative ideas for raising kids to know and love God / Wayne Rice.
    p. cm.
  Includes bibliographical references and index.
  ISBN 978-0-7847-2125-4
  1. Christian education--Home training. 2. Christian education of children. I. Title.
  BV1590.R53 2010
  248.8'45--dc22
                          2009053005

15 14 13 12 11 10   2 3 4 5 6 7 8 9 10

❧ CONTENTS ❧

❧ CHALLENGE ❧

Tim Davis and his wife, Sherrie, are first-generation Christians who **want to give their children something they never had—a Christian home.** After hearing their pastor speak enthusiastically about the benefits of family devotions, they decided to give it a try—Bible reading and prayer after dinner every night. Things went great, or at least good, the first couple of weeks, but soon the kids started complaining about how boring it all was and how they would rather do something else, even homework! With family devotions becoming more of a burden for their family than a benefit, Tim and Sherrie gave up on them. They're still trying to figure out what it means to have a Christian home.

Rosie Morales has two children, both boys, ages nine and seven. Three years ago she started going to church; she was hoping to find a social group for single moms. At a women's retreat last year, she gave her life to Christ and has been growing in her faith ever since. She **wants her sons to know Jesus too and to find some Christian friends,** but her ex-husband gets the boys on weekends and won't allow them to attend her church. He doesn't want the boys to become "Jesus freaks" like their mother.

Dan Morgan comes from a long line of Scottish Presbyterians who helped establish churches all over New England. Both his father and grandfather were pastors, and it was pretty much expected that Dan would follow in their footsteps. But he chose a career in the financial services industry and now has a successful job on Wall Street. He lives in New Jersey with his wife, Judith, and their three children, fifteen, twelve, and ten. "I don't get to spend much time with my kids," he laments, a reference to his long commute to work and the late hours he spends at the office. Dan also rarely has time to attend church but **wants his children to have the same legacy of faith that his parents left for him.** This year, he donated a large amount of money to the church so that a new youth minister could be hired. He's hoping this will help get his kids more involved in the church.

Jim and Denise Tompkins *have four children at home—two from Denise's previous marriage and two who were born since their marriage five years ago. Jim also has a teenage daughter who lives with her mother, Jim's first wife. Denise was raised in a Christian home and Jim was led to Christ by a friend at his job after the breakup of his first marriage.* **Recently they've been quite concerned about their oldest, sixteen-year-old Kristina, who has been experimenting with drugs and has run away from home twice.** *They've tried making her go to church, but they're afraid of the impact this is having on their younger children, who may be starting to think of church attendance as punishment. They aren't sure what to do.*

Derek and Janine Miller *try hard to* **protect their children from worldly influences.** *They homeschool their kids and severely restrict their exposure to television, the Internet, and other forms of entertainment and electronic media. Recently their twelve-year-old son, Jared, asked for permission to attend Revolution, an outreach event sponsored by their church's youth ministry that features hip-hop music and skateboarders with tattoos. Their refusal to allow Jared to go has created something of a crisis in their family. Now the Millers* **are considering changing churches.**

If you're a Christian parent like me, you can probably identify with one or more of the parents in these stories. Your family may be quite different, but you can understand what these parents are feeling and experiencing.

That's because as Christian parents we have at least two things in common.

First, we care deeply about the spiritual lives of our children. More than anything else, we want our kids to have faith in Christ and to walk with God for the rest of their lives. We want them to follow in our footsteps and raise a Christian family of their own. We want them to meet us in Heaven someday.

But we have a second thing in common as well. We aren't sure any of those things will happen. We don't know what we're doing most of the time. We feel incompetent and insecure. We worry that we don't have the time to teach our children. We worry that our kids are being influenced more by their friends and the entertainment industry than by us. We've tried leading family devotions only to see them degenerate into fights. We've taken our kids to church only to get grumbling and complaining. We compare our kids with other people's kids and feel guilt, disappointment, or embarrassment. We worry that our kids are wandering away from the faith. We worry if they'll ever come back.

Welcome to the world of Christian parenting. As any believing parent will tell you, there is no greater joy than watching your children grow strong in their faith and leading them to Christ. But along with the joy comes frustration, struggle, and a sense of inadequacy that has challenged and discouraged every parent since Adam and Eve. If you don't feel qualified to lead your children in the footsteps of faith, you're in good company. Every parent has felt exactly the same way.

We aren't sure any of those things will happen.
We don't know what we're doing most of the time.

no guarantees

When my wife, Marci, and I became parents for the first time almost forty years ago, we assumed that children who grow up in Christian homes likely become Christians themselves. At least, that was our experience. Our parents were faithful Christians, as were their parents before them. Christianity was part of our DNA—or so we thought. We had every reason to believe that if we trained up our children "in the way [they] should go" (Proverbs 22:6), they would indeed go that way, even if they strayed for a short time, which we know teenagers frequently do.

We've since learned that there are no guarantees in the Bible—or anywhere else, for that matter—concerning the raising of children. Truth is, you can do everything right and still see your children walk away from their faith when they get older. And despite all that you've been led to believe, they may never come back—at least not during your lifetime. That's because every child eventually grows up to become an adult with a mind of his or her own. You can't control your children or the choices they make. That doesn't mean we shouldn't do all we can do to lead our children to Christ, to teach them the truth of God's Word, and to provide them a home where Christian values are demonstrated day in and day out. It just means that we have no control over outcomes. Our children are not us.

If your goal as a parent is to raise trophy children who follow in your footsteps so that you can brag on them and feel successful as a parent, then you are setting yourself up for a big disappointment. While what you do as a parent matters, you're not the one who determines what your children ultimately believe or how they choose to live their lives. Only they can decide those things—as we all must do. God wouldn't have it any other way, and neither should we.

It should come as no surprise that many young people who were raised in devout Christian homes turn their backs on the faith of their childhood as adults. Just because they went to a Christian school, attended church, memorized Bible verses, and said all the right things . . . none of these behaviors guarantee that they'll have faith as adults. When our children do all the right things and say all the right things as children, it's possible that what we really may be getting are false positives. They may look good on the outside, but something is missing on the inside.

I've often wondered why some young people remain strong in their faith while others fall away. There are no simple answers to that question, of course, but there's no question that parents are in a better position to influence their children than anybody or *anything* else; I'm going to talk much more about that in this book. It's not about making sure our children are involved in the right church or the very best youth group. It's about what's happening at home. When parents are consistently and passionately involved in the spiritual formation of their children, the odds go up tremendously that the children will follow in their parents' footsteps.

If your goal as a parent is to raise trophy children who follow in your footsteps so that you can brag on them and feel successful as a parent, then you are setting yourself up for a big disappointment.

This is not a book on how to make your kids behave like Christians. This is a book on how to behave as parents. What we do matters. There is a puzzling paradox here, of course. Only God can draw children to himself (John 6:44). Yet he depends on us to teach our children (Deuteronomy 6:7) and to provide for them the kind of environment that will produce faith (Ephesians 6:4). In a very real sense, we are in a partnership with God, providing for our children the foundation on which faith is built.

God has always done his best work through people and he has chosen to work through parents rather than pastors and programs to produce faith in children. Every child must find his or her own way to faith, but God has appointed you to serve as a means of grace through which he draws your children to himself. Your faithfulness as a parent makes it possible for your kids to encounter God's love, to accept Christ as Savior, and to make him Lord of their lives.

no formulas

If you're looking for a secret formula or a step-by-step blueprint for raising godly kids, this book is not going to provide that for you. Despite what you may have heard, there isn't one particular style of parenting that the Bible endorses.

Truth is, you can't find many examples of good parenting in the Bible. While the Bible does offer some good parenting advice, most of the families we read about in the Bible have all kinds of problems. It's unfortunate that in the church we often give the impression that there is an ideal mom and dad and one way to raise children. It's also easy to believe that this ideal way is modeled after families from nostalgic TV sitcoms like *Leave It to Beaver* or *The Cosby Show*—and what the Bible has to say often doesn't enter our equation.

Don't worry. You don't have to be like that family that homeschools their kids, or the one that sits together in the front row of your church every Sunday, or the one that doesn't allow its kids to listen to anything but contemporary Christian music or watch any TV, except for maybe *The Andy Griffith Show*.

There is no *one way* to raise godly children. My goal in this book is not to unveil a one-size-fits-all curriculum for teaching the Christian faith to your kids, nor is it to produce cookie-cutter Christians who all believe and behave the same way. Instead, I hope to provide you with a biblical framework and lots of practical ideas (and they are only *ideas*, simply places to start) to create your own way of passing faith on to your kids. You don't have to do it the same way my family does it—or anyone else's.

There are three things to keep in mind while you're reading this book.

First, your family is unique. It's not like any other family. No two families are alike, not even families from the same church that live in the same neighborhood. Some families are large, some are small; some have two parents, some have one; some are blended, some are not; some are loud, some are quiet; some are busy, some like more simple ways; some have assertive, strong-willed kids, some have assertive, strong-willed parents; some are dysfunctional, and some are even *more* dysfunctional.

And yours may be none of the above.

That's OK. While I will do some generalizing about families and parents in this book, you'll need to be discerning about how you apply the principles and ideas on these pages. Not everything will apply or be appropriate for you and your family because your family is unique.

Second, your children are unique. If you're a parent, you know the truth of that statement. Your kids are each very different from each other and from other people's kids, and here's another shocker: they're not like you, either. You can't make them be you, or be what you always wanted to be. The biblical instruction to "train a child in the way he should go" (Proverbs 22:6) suggests that children have a particular bent—the way that God created them to be raised. Our job as parents is to train children in the same way that a gardener trains a vine or branch to maximize its growth potential and bring out its natural beauty.

Parents who've raised more than one child know this is true. Just because you raise all of your children in the same house with the same parents and the same faith doesn't mean they'll all believe or behave the same. Truth is, that rarely happens. Marci and I have raised three children and watched each of them choose their own unique spiritual identities. We can't explain any of that except to acknowledge that they are each very different people with different ways of understanding and responding to God.

Just because you raise all of your children in the same house with the same parents and the same faith doesn't mean they'll all believe or behave the same. Truth is, that rarely happens.

Third, your spiritual journey is unique. While we share a common faith in Christ, I think we all can agree that the Christian family is a large one. None of us is in the same place spiritually, nor do we all affirm or express our faith in the same way. For that reason, this book will not prescribe a particular theological point of view or a set of creeds for you to teach your children. Of course, you'll want to be clear with your children about what you believe and why you believe it (we'll spend some time discussing that in chapter four), but I'm not going to tell you what to teach. That's entirely up to you. Remember that you can't give your kids your exact faith, my faith, or anyone else's faith. What you *can* give them is what is authentic and real to you.

no regrets

My experience has been that as you get older you tend not to regret the things you did as much as the things you did *not* do. My hope in writing this book is that you will look back on the efforts you made to lead your children to walk with God and have no regrets.

You may be a first-generation Christian or you may have been raised in a Christian home. You may have children who are very young or you may have teenagers who are almost grown. Your children may have one parent, two parents, or many parents. They may be doing very well spiritually or they may be far from God. You may feel relatively confident as the spiritual leader of your home or, like the parents I described at the start, you may be struggling with how to help your children walk with God.

Regardless of your religious background, your knowledge of the Bible, or your parenting experience, you have all you need to become the primary spiritual influence and caregiver for your children. The fact that you've picked up this book says a lot about your willingness to become the parent God wants you to be. That's all that matters. *The important thing is that you begin now.* I trust that this book will encourage you, motivate you, and equip you with some helpful ideas and resources that will help you take advantage of the strategic position you've been given by God to lead your children forward in the footsteps of faith—generation after generation.

🌿 🌿 🌿 🌿

This book would not have been possible without the example of my parents, John F. and Mary C. (Kay) Rice, who taught me to love Jesus from the time I was old enough to love anything at all. When I was only five, they perched me on the altar of the little Nazarene church in Oxnard, California, where I sang a verse and chorus of "He Lives" in front of the whole church—a song I have not stopped singing and one that defines me to this day. Mom and Dad did a wonderful job of leaving a spiritual legacy for me and my siblings—my two brothers, Jim and Joe, and my sister, Mary. I'd also like to thank my stepfather, Rush Birdwell, who has graciously loved my mother for forty years after the untimely death of my father and who not only strengthened our family's legacy of faith but also added considerably to it.

Thank you, Marci, for loving me so well for so many years and for teaching me by your example so much of what I have tried to convey in this book. Nathan, Amber, and Corey, you have been a great blessing to me, and my prayer for each of you is that you will continue to love and serve God and to pass your legacy of faith on to our beautiful grandchildren.

The outline for this book and much of its content was originally developed for a parent seminar that is presented in churches all over North America by a ministry team called HomeWord, now affiliated with Azusa Pacific University. I want to thank all the members of the HomeWord seminar team, especially David Lynn and Tim Smith, for their good ideas and assistance on this project. Thanks also to Greg Johnson at WordServe Literary Group and Bob Irvin at Standard Publishing for encouraging me to write this book and bringing it to fruition.

This book is dedicated to HomeWord's founder, Jim Burns, my good friend, who has been a great inspiration and encouragement to me over the years.

Wayne Rice
Lakeside, California

commission

*J*enny! We're going to be late!

But Mom, why do I have to go to church? None of my friends have to go!

I don't care what your friends don't have to do. Let's GO!

I told you, I don't want to go! Church is boring!

Get in the car! You're not staying home!

I hate church! You can't make me go!

Another discouraging Sunday morning at the Robinson home. Rick and Dana are on the verge of giving up, spiritually, on their fifteen-year-old daughter, Jenny.

Jenny wasn't always this way. As a child, she loved going to church. In fact, there was hardly a time when she didn't go to church. Her earliest memories are of going to Sunday school, hearing adventure-filled stories from the Bible, and singing silly songs with catchy tunes and crazy hand motions. She participated in all the children's programs and, as she got older, was an active member and leader of the junior high youth group.

Now a sophomore in high school, Jenny has changed. She's lost interest in church as her attention has turned to boys, clothes, music, the popular online networking sites, school, and seemingly endless extracurricular activities that pull her farther and farther away from her family and the faith of her childhood.

Rick and Dana aren't sure what to do. Do they force Jenny to go to church? Do they give up? Should they change churches? Should they send her away to some kind of Christian boarding school or boot camp? Do they seek professional help? They've considered these and many other possibilities.

The Robinson family can trace their family's faith back several generations. Both Rick and Dana grew up in Christian homes. Rick's father was an elder in the church and Dana's parents were missionaries. Church attendance was mandatory when they were children, and they have no memory of ever arguing over this issue with their parents like Jenny argues with them. Jenny's apparent rejection of the family heritage has become a heavy burden for Rick and Dana to bear. They love their daughter and, more than anything in the world, want her to follow in their footsteps—the footsteps of faith.

They have no memory of ever arguing over this issue with their parents like Jenny argues with them. Jenny's apparent rejection of the family heritage has become a heavy burden for Rick and Dana to bear.

Rick and Dana are not unlike thousands of Christian parents today who are hurting because their children appear to be walking away from the faith of their childhood. The growing percentage of youth who are leaving the church as they reach late adolescence has become a serious concern not only for parents but also for youth ministry professionals nearly everywhere. According to a study conducted in 2007, 70 percent of young adults ages twenty-three to thirty say they stopped attending church between the ages of eighteen and twenty-two. Researcher Ed Stetzer noted: "There is no easy way to say it, but it must be said. Parents and churches are not passing on a robust Christian faith and an accompanying commitment to the church. . . . [We] have to ask the hard question, 'What is it about our faith commitment that does not find root in the lives of our children?'"[1] Ironically, this is taking place even as our churches have grown in the size of their budgets, their buildings, their staffs, and their programs. What's going on?

We certainly can't fault Rick and Dana for wanting Jenny to go to church. After all, they want their daughter to have a personal faith that is strong and secure—to believe what they believe, to know Christ as they do, and to obediently walk with God. That's what every Christian parent wants for his or her children.

Ironically, this is taking place even as our churches have grown in the size of their budgets, their buildings, their staffs, and their programs. What's going on?

But maybe Rick and Dana have made the same mistake many parents make today. They've bought into the notion that the church exists to do this job for them—that they can somehow *outsource* the Christian education and spiritual care of their children to paid professionals. Just as they send their children to school to get an education, so they take their children to church to learn about God. It seems to make sense in today's busy world, which has specialists for nearly everything.

But we've learned from experience as well as research on this subject that faith just doesn't get passed on that way. While the church plays an important and positive role in the faith development of our children, it can't provide the kind of environment from which faith takes root and flourishes. The church is a wonderful place for children to learn *about* the Christian faith, but the home is the best place for children to *encounter* the love and grace of God, which can only be experienced in caring, long-term relationships. That's where we're going in this book.

whose job is it anyway?

All three of my children went to church every Sunday from the time they were born until the time they went away to college. Regular and frequent church attendance was something of a defining characteristic of our family life and more or less a nonnegotiable house rule. We faithfully attended church as a family because we wanted our kids to understand the importance of putting God first. Going to church on Sunday rather than doing other things we like to do was one of the ways we taught our children this important priority.

Still, we learned over the years that the church is very limited in what it can do. It provided us with a wonderful place to worship together as a family, to participate in all kinds of age-appropriate programs and activities, to hear some great preaching and teaching, to connect with friends and enjoy fellowship with other believers, to serve in a variety of worthwhile ministries, and a whole lot more. But the church never provided for our children the environment, the people, or the programs capable of making disciples of our kids. That's not a knock on any of the churches we attended as a family. They were all wonderful churches full of incredible people and our grown kids have many fond memories of them. My point is that the church was never given the responsibility for making disciples of my kids, your kids, or anyone else's kids. God in his infinite wisdom gave that responsibility exclusively to parents. Any religious institution that thinks it has the authority to raise your children is probably a cult, not a church.

The relevant scripture is found in Deuteronomy 6:

Love the Lord your God with all your heart and with all your soul and with all your strength. These commandments that I give you today are to be upon your hearts. Impress them on your children. Talk about them when you sit at home and when you walk along the road, when you lie down and when you get up (vv. 5-7).

I'm also a fan of how *The Message* version renders these verses:

Love GOD, your GOD, with your whole heart: love him with all that's in you, love him with all you've got! Write these commandments that I've given you today on your hearts. Get them inside of you and then get them inside your children. Talk about them wherever you are, sitting at home or walking in the street; talk about them from the time you get up in the morning to when you fall into bed at night (vv. 5-7).

Any religious institution that thinks it has the authority to raise your children is probably a cult, not a church.

Obviously these words weren't written to "the church." When Moses wrote these words from God, he didn't write them for the priests or religious leaders of the day. He wrote them to *parents*—the only ones who could possibly talk about the commandments of God at home from the time children woke up to the time they went to bed. This is confirmed in Psalm 78:

We will not hide them from their children;

we will tell the next generation the praiseworthy deeds of the Lord . . .

He decreed statutes for Jacob

and established the law in Israel,

which he commanded our forefathers

to teach their children,

so the next generation would know them,

even the children yet to be born,

and they in turn would tell their children (vv. 4-6).

Parents in ancient Hebrew times were well aware of their commission to pass the faith along from one generation to the next. They took it quite literally and taught their children the words of Deuteronomy 6 (what is called the Shema) every day—several times a day, in fact, just as the Scriptures instructed them to do. In fact, these verses may be the most quoted verses in the entire Bible, when all faiths are considered. They are still recited daily in many Jewish homes today just as they were at the time of Moses.

Unless one generation of believers tells the next about the love of God and the good news of the gospel, it won't get passed on at all.

A Christian doesn't believe in a legalistic or mechanical application of the Old Testament law, but the spirit of the law remains true and applicable to our lives today. There's no question that God wants parents to be actively involved in the daily religious instruction of their children.

You may be thinking, *Oh great. It's hard enough teaching my kids to eat green beans, let alone love God. Don't we as parents have enough to do?* Certainly that's a legitimate concern. Parents have a lot on their plates already, and this may seem like an unfair burden that God has placed on your shoulders. You probably didn't sign up to become your child's Sunday school teacher.

But God's commission to parents in Deuteronomy 6 was never meant to turn you into a Sunday school teacher, nor was it meant to be a burden. It was meant to be a blessing. Why should someone else get the privilege and joy of leading your child to Christ? The book of Psalms reminds us that "your statutes are wonderful; therefore I obey them" (Psalm 119:129). There are many verses in the Bible just like that one. It's almost as if God knew we would grumble, so he keeps reminding us that his laws and commands are for our own benefit. That's especially true for Deuteronomy 6. There is no greater joy for a Christian parent than leading a child to Christ and seeing him or her grow in faith and become a Christ-follower for life. I believe God wants that for every parent.

> ### ❧ GRAB A KID AND GO ❧
>
> OK, you need to make a trip to the hardware store to pick up a few nuts and bolts, PVC pipe, and duct tape. Fifteen minutes there and fifteen minutes back.
>
> You're not thinking of going by yourself, are you?
>
> This is a perfect time for a little one-on-one with one of the kids. "Hey Luke, want to make a trip to the hardware store with me?" By taking your child with you on errands like this, you'll get his or her full attention and they will get yours. Do you need to talk about spiritual things or use some things that happen as teachable moments? If the occasion arises, sure. But probably not. This is one of those relationship-building times that come for free—unless you decide to add in a stop for ice cream on the way home, which isn't a bad idea—along with some surprising possibilities for good conversation.

why parents?

It has been said that Christianity is only one generation away from extinction, which may sound like an exaggeration. But it's literally true. The Christian faith doesn't get passed on from one generation to the next by the mass media, by organizations, or by programs—it happens through people. Unless one generation of believers tells the next about the love of God and the good news of the gospel, it won't get passed on at all.

There have been previous generations that have failed to take this responsibility seriously. In the book of Judges, there's a revealing paragraph about Joshua's descendants, which reads:

After that whole generation had been gathered to their fathers, another generation grew up, who knew neither the Lord nor what he had done for Israel. Then the Israelites did evil in the eyes of the Lord and served the Baals. They forsook the Lord, the God of their fathers, who had brought them out of Egypt. They followed and worshiped various gods of the peoples around them. They provoked the Lord to anger because they forsook him and served Baal and the Ashtoreths. In his anger against Israel the Lord handed them over to raiders who plundered them. He sold them to their enemies all around, whom they were no longer able to resist. Whenever Israel went out to fight, the hand of the Lord was against them to defeat them, just as he had sworn to them. They were in great distress (Judges 2:10-15).

We're naive to think that this same scenario couldn't happen today. Truth is, we're seeing it happen in some parts of the world. Beautiful cathedrals that were erected centuries ago for the purpose of worship and praise to God have been turned into tourist attractions—monuments to an entire generation of Christians who failed to take this commission seriously and leave for their children a legacy of faith.

Still, God continues to rely on parents to get it done. Because the world has changed so much, we sometimes think that maybe some of those old biblical texts are no longer relevant or somehow no longer apply to us. But here's what the Bible itself says about that:

FAMILY SERVICE PROJECTS

FAMILY PRAYERS

❧ NEWSPAPER PRAYERS ❧

Here's an easy way to get your children to think spiritually with the new day. Take the morning newspaper—or, if you get all your news online, pull up a few key stories for them—and ask your kids to go through the paper, or the stories, looking for things you can pray for as a family. After you pray, choose one of those things that you might be able to get involved with as a family. Perhaps someone's house burned down or was broken into. Do some research to find out if there is some way to help. Doing a simple thing like taking old clothes or a meal to this family will help them greatly—and impact your kids for a long time.

What you say goes, GOD,

and stays, as permanent as the heavens.

Your truth never goes out of fashion;

it's as up-to-date as the earth when the sun comes up (Psalm 119:89, 90, The Message).

God hasn't changed his basic strategy for passing on the faith. He still wants parents to do it one-on-one with their children, pretty much like the people of ancient Israel did, using conversations, stories, and the normal routines of family life. In reality, it's a strategy that still makes perfect sense. Here are a few reasons why.

No one has more influence on children than parents. If you find this hard to believe, you're not alone. That's why so much research has been done on this subject over the past forty years. The National Study of Youth and Religion, the largest, most comprehensive study on the religious and spiritual lives of American youth to date, was conducted by the University of North Carolina to determine who or what has the greatest influence on the formation of adolescent faith and values. Christian Smith, one of the study researchers, came to this conclusion: "Contrary to popular misguided cultural stereotypes and frequent parental misperceptions . . . the evidence clearly shows that the single most important social influence on the religious and spiritual lives of adolescents is their parents."[2]

Beautiful cathedrals that were erected centuries ago for the purpose of worship and praise to God have been turned into tourist attractions— monuments to an entire generation of Christians who failed to take this commission seriously.

This, of course, flies in the face of the common view that peers and popular culture are the most powerful influencers of today's young people. Perhaps the reason for this view is that for many of today's kids, this *is* true. In today's world of busy parents, electronic babysitters, and unrelenting competition from popular culture and the entertainment media, more and more kids are growing up without the kind of caring adult relationships that can positively influence them. When parents are absent or when they simply choose not to take advantage of the influence they have, kids are left to the influences of whomever or whatever they spend most of their time with. This is not influence that is inevitable or can't be overcome by parents or other caring adults such as grandparents and mentors. But to not address it is to simply give up your influence by default.

Yes, there are many influences on children and teenagers today—perhaps more now than ever. But the influence of a parent—no matter how good or bad—has more power to shape a child's beliefs and behavior than any other.

No one has more time with children than parents. It takes time to instill faith and values in children and no one has more time with a child than a parent does. Pastors, Sunday school teachers, youth workers, children's workers—they are with your children one or two hours a week . . . maybe. But in all likelihood you're with them every day for much of the day. When God commissioned parents to be the primary spiritual caregivers for children, he knew that, with few exceptions, parents would have more time to be with them than anyone else.

It all starts when your children are born, of course. Who else besides parents are with children from the day they are born? Children are not born with an automatic, inbred faith. Their default setting is to selfishness—the curse

---

FAMILY DINNERS

❧ MAD-SAD-GLAD ❧

Here's one especially good for smaller kids, but the big ones will have fun with it if they play along with the younger ones as well (and you, as the parent, are fully engaged too!). At dinnertime, or anytime you want to get some good conversation going, play a little game of "Mad-Sad-Glad." Just ask everyone to share something that made them *mad* that day (or during the past week), something that made them *sad*, and something that made them *glad*. Follow this up with a time of prayer for each other.

FAMILY DEVOTION IDEA

❧ LETTERS TO GOD ❧

For a family devotion, have your children write letters to God. They can be letters of praise, letters of thanksgiving, letters of request, or letters of inquiry (questions they have). Once their letters are written, they can be "sent" by reading them out loud as a family to God.

that all of us take from our first parents, Adam and Eve. Children don't automatically turn into good kids, as every parent knows. From a very early age, children have to be taught about goodness and they must be taught about God. Otherwise, they're likely to head down the wrong road, the widest of roads, the one that Jesus called "the road that leads to destruction" (Matthew 7:13).

God tells parents to have faith conversations "when you sit at home and when you walk along the road, when you lie down and when you get up" . . . in other words, all the time. Parents are the only ones who can do that. If you don't think you have enough time to do this with your kids, who has more? The answer is *nobody*.

True faith doesn't happen because a child has attended a lot of Sunday school classes or Vacation Bible Schools or watched a lot of Christian videos. True faith comes as the result of a caring relationship over time that can best be provided by parents.

No one has more love for children than parents. As a youth worker in the church for many years, I can honestly say I've loved the students I've worked with in my youth groups. That's a given of youth ministry. If you

---

FAMILY DEVOTION IDEAS

DEVOTIONS ON LOCATION

Try having your family devotions or prayer times in a number of different places. Think of different areas you can go to near where you live. Sometimes the location itself will suggest a Bible passage to study together or something to pray for. Some ideas:

- In a park or garden—Jesus often prayed in a garden
- On a roof—there are many passages of Scripture having to do with roofs or rooftops, such as when a man was lowered through a roof to be healed by Jesus in Mark 2, or when Peter was praying on the roof in Acts 10
- By a pool—Jesus healed people by the pool of Bethesda in John 5; pray for people you know who are sick or need healing in some way
- In a car
- By (or up in!) a tree
- At the beach
- On a boat
- In the basement
- On the roof of a tall building, such as a parking garage
- In the dark (there are spiritual lessons you can talk about with this one, for sure!)
- At the zoo (some time talking about Noah and his ark, anyone?)
- In a gym
- At a landfill
- On a mountain
- In a cave
- At a homeless shelter
- More ideas that you have!

don't love teens you can't be a very effective youth worker.

But I've *never* loved a kid in my youth group like I've loved (and still love) my own children. There's absolutely no comparison. No one on earth loves your children more than you do. No one cares what happens to them more than you do. Parental love is so strong that Jesus often compared God's love to the love of a human father. God's love is greater, of course, but everyone can understand the kind of love that would cause a father to sit on his front porch for days on end patiently waiting for his son to come home. Love like that is compelling and a vivid illustration of God's love for us.

> **FAMILY TRADITIONS**
>
> **❧ UNCONDITIONAL LOVE ❧**
>
> Establish a tradition in your home that no one can go to bed until they've told each member of the family "I love you." As simple as can be, right? But extremely powerful.

Just remember that God gave you this assignment not because you have a lot of Bible knowledge or because you have the perfect family or even because you are particularly reliable and trustworthy. He chose you because you love your kids far more than anyone else does!

The most influence, the most time, the most love. God definitely knew what he was doing when he gave parents not only the responsibility, but also the great privilege, of loving and leading his children into a personal relationship with himself.

"yes buts"

But it's not that simple, is it? If you're like many parents, knowing all this doesn't make you feel better, and it may make you feel worse! You feel even more guilty, even more inadequate. You may believe that God has commissioned parents to be the spiritual leaders of their families, but you have a hard time believing that he would expect *you* to take on this responsibility. In a perfect world you could do it, but the world isn't perfect and neither are you! Like many parents, you may have some questions, concerns, or very good reasons—"yes buts"—that are holding you back.

Believe me, I understand. I've had a few "yes buts" of my own that kept me from being the spiritual leader in my home that I should have been. Some of them are on the list below. Grab a pen or pencil and put a check beside those that have been a concern for you.

- ❑ "The job seems so big; I just don't know where to begin."
- ❑ "I'm not spiritual enough."
- ❑ "I have no training in the Bible or theology."
- ❑ "I don't have the gift of teaching."
- ❑ "My spouse and I come from different religious backgrounds."
- ❑ "We have a blended family."
- ❑ "I'm a single parent."
- ❑ "I don't have the time."
- ❑ "My children have disabilities or special needs."
- ❑ "My children go to a Christian school and attend church. They need a break from religion when they get home."
- ❑ "I tried before but gave up on it."
- ❑ "My kids aren't comfortable discussing spiritual things with me."
- ❑ "I'll start doing it . . . someday."
- ❑ "My kids seem to be doing fine so far."
- ❑ "My kids are teenagers or young adults. It's too late."
- ❑ _____
- ❑ _____
- ❑ _____

So how did you do? Most people check off about five or six. Maybe you have a "yes but" or two that are not even on this list. Go ahead, write them down, and don't be discouraged! Remember that the first step to overcoming barriers like these is to simply admit that they exist. Then you can begin to deal with them.

Let me take the "yes buts" on this list one at a time and offer a few words of encouragement.

"The job seems so big; I just don't know where to begin." This is a common frustration. Sometimes we get paralyzed by what seems to be the immensity of a task. It's reasonable to expect that leading your children to walk with God is not something you'll be able to complete in a few days or even a few years. So the temptation is to keep putting it off. As an author, I know that feeling well. The hardest part of a book to write is the first paragraph.

The disciples of Jesus surely felt that way when they heard the growling stomachs of five thousand people who came to hear Jesus. The sheer size of the problem prevented them from taking any action at all. But finally a little boy volunteered his lunch, a few loaves and a few fish. "How far can this possibly go?" asked Andrew, maybe being a little too honest. And of course, you know the rest of the story.

It would be very discouraging if we looked in the Bible and found only perfect parents raising perfect kids or bad parents raising bad kids. It doesn't work that way.

When I have a big job to do, I have to remind myself that *something is always better than nothing.* What I do doesn't have to be perfect; it doesn't have to be complete. It just has to be *something.* What I need to do is take a few steps—even one or two small ones—that are possible today to move toward my ultimate goal. We'll discuss goals in chapter two, but remember that if your goal is to feed five thousand people, it might be a good idea to start with someone who has a lunch he is willing to share. More will be done through that one than through a thousand others who throw up their hands in despair.

Reading a book like this one, and challenging yourself to take responsibility for your children's spiritual growth, can be intimidating and guilt-producing for sure. This book will have dozens of ideas and principles that parents just like you have used to lead their children to walk with God. All of them have the potential to discourage you as well as give you hope. *Just remember that you don't have to do them all.* In fact, you really don't have to do any of them. What you need to do is *something* and that something may not even be in this book at all! Start small; begin with what makes sense to you and works for you. Eventually, you may find that you've done a lot more than you thought. What you do may not seem very impressive, but watch what happens when you let God have it. He still knows how to turn a lunch into a banquet.

"I'm not spiritual enough." If you don't feel like your relationship with God is all that it could be, you're in good company. A closer look at the heroes of our faith—people like Moses, Elijah, Peter, and Paul—reveals that all of them went through difficult times of doubt, questioning, sinfulness, or spiritual dryness. David, for one, was very transparent about his spiritual struggles and shortcomings: "O my God, I cry out by day, but you do not answer . . . I confess my iniquity; I am troubled by my sin" (Psalm 22:2, 38:18). Still, the Bible says that David was "a man after [God's] own heart" (1 Samuel 13:14).

If I've learned anything after forty-plus years of ministry, it's that God uses very imperfect "jars of clay" (2 Corinthians 4:7) to do his work in the world. I've been privileged to spend time with many mentors and heroes, men and women who are often regarded as spiritual giants. Even though they've helped me and thousands of others grow spiritually through their speaking and writing, I've learned they aren't perfect. They are often flawed, with insecurities, bad habits, doubts, and struggles just like yours and mine. But that hasn't disqualified them from being able to teach the truth with passion and authority.

It would be very discouraging if we looked in the Bible and found only perfect parents raising perfect kids or bad parents raising bad kids. It doesn't work that way. There are very few examples in the Bible of parents who raised spiritual giants because they were spiritual giants themselves. Adam and Eve, who walked with God as the first created man and woman, had the first dysfunctional family—one son murdered another—and every family since has followed suit. There are no perfect parents in the Bible because all of them are human parents, just like we are. God can use anyone to raise good kids. Jesus' family tree (Matthew 1), which is full of scoundrels, is a testament to that truth.

Your children don't require parents who have it all together. Obviously, you want to practice what you preach, but none of us do that perfectly. If you want to lead your children to walk with God, the best thing you can do is do all you can to stay on the road yourself and walk alongside them. Keep learning and growing. Your example will always speak louder than words. We'll discuss this more in the next chapter, but for now remember that you can't lead your children where you yourself are not willing to go. It's OK to not feel as spiritual as you would like to be, but if you're seeking God yourself and growing, even slowly, in your faith and walk with God, you're going to do just fine. This is the basic formula needed to provide your kids with the spiritual leadership they need.

"I have no training in the Bible or theology." So you're not a Bible expert? No problem. When God gave parents his commission in Deuteronomy 6 to "teach these things" to their children, he also reduced "these things" down to a couple of sentences. *There is only one God. Love him with all your heart, mind, and soul.* That's basically it. And Jesus summarized the whole Bible in a similar way: *Love God. Love people* (Matthew 22:36-40). Anyone can teach those things to their children in simple yet profound ways. There's no need to overcomplicate what you teach your children, especially at first.

You don't need to be a theologian, Bible scholar, or have years of Christianity under your belt to lead your children to walk with God. You do need to be learning yourself and working on your own relationship with God so that you stay in step with your children, or, hopefully, a step or two ahead of them. But you'll be surprised at how much you learn as you begin this journey together with your kids. What a great opportunity you'll have to deepen your knowledge of the Bible as you help your children learn. Today there are plenty of fantastic resources available that can help you add more content to all that you're teaching your children. Some of those resources will be provided for you later in this book.

> FAMILY DEVOTIONS
>
> ❧ NATURE HIKE DEVOTIONS ❧
>
> Struggling with that feeling of not knowing how to teach? Let nature teach for you! Go on a nature hike and have devotions at a place where you can see some of God's creation—on the beach, on a mountain, along a stream, around a campfire. All you have to do is spend some time thanking God for his creation and enjoy some time together as a family.

"I don't have the gift of teaching." Some parents are terrified at the prospect of having to teach their children because they don't feel qualified as a teacher.

But here's good news for all of us: God rarely appoints people to do something based on their qualifications. Take Moses: he was commanded by God to go into Egypt and make a very important speech to Pharaoh. Moses objected on the grounds that he was a lousy speaker. "I am slow of speech," he reminded God, possibly stuttering as he said it. God's answer to Moses is relevant to us today. In so many words, what God told Moses was: "I invented your mouth and I will put the right words in it. Now get moving—and remember that I will be with you the whole time" (Exodus 4:10-12).

Just as you don't need to be a spiritual giant or a Bible scholar, you don't need the gift of teaching to teach your children about God. All you really need is God.

"My spouse and I come from different religious backgrounds." If you and your spouse come from different *Christian* religious backgrounds—Protestant and Catholic, for example—there is still a lot of common ground that you can affirm together as a couple to teach your children. Obviously, you'll have to decide which church to attend together and which traditions you want your children to experience and embrace, but there's no reason you can't give your children a positive home environment where they can learn about the love of God. Leading children to walk with God should not be a competition between parents. The key is to work together with your spouse to accomplish this goal.

Of course, if you and your spouse are from very different religious backgrounds without a common view of the Bible or of essential Christian beliefs, then you'll have a greater challenge for sure. If your spouse is not a Christian or is of another faith entirely, you'll want to be respectful of his or her views and avoid creating even more division in your home. Don't allow your children to be caught in a religious tug-of-war. My advice is to go slow and know that even small demonstrations of the Christian faith in front of your children can be used powerfully by God to lead children to Christ. This book will provide you with a number of ideas. I've known many young people who became Christians through the example of just one parent who loved Jesus with humility and grace.

"We have a blended family." Like all families, blended families come with their own unique sets of challenges. Just like families with more than one religious background, blended families bring a variety of heritages, backgrounds, personalities, and living situations to the table. None of these things have to become insurmountable obstacles; in fact, they can become incredible opportunities for uniting the family under the banner of Christian love. There's absolutely nothing more unifying than having everyone in the family loving and serving the same Lord. Love that goes vertically spreads horizontally. I think this diagram helps illustrate what I mean.

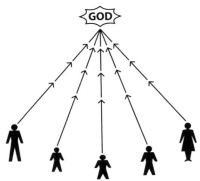

As each member of the family gets closer to God (vertical), the closer each member of the family gets to each other (horizontal). It may not actually happen quite as simply or easily as the diagram makes it look, but the principle is nonetheless true. Blended families, which often come with some degree of brokenness, can find healing and an increased sense of unity when the focus is on God and not on themselves.

Don't think that blended families are a problem for God. He is very familiar with the problems of blended and broken families. He even put Jesus in one. Mary and Joseph's family was by no means traditional. God is well equipped to help restore broken and strained relationships, but he needs our cooperation and willingness to participate with him in the process. It all starts with you.

Leading children to walk with God should not be a competition between parents. The key is to work together with your spouse to accomplish this goal.

"I'm a single parent." It's estimated that one in four children today grow up in single parent homes, usually headed by mothers. Single moms and single dads have difficult challenges to overcome. But children can be influenced just as positively by one parent as two. Nowhere does the Bible require two parents to raise godly kids. The book of Ecclesiastes does say that "two are better than one," but a few verses later it also says, in so many words, that three are better than two (Ecclesiastes 4:9, 12)! In other words, the Bible encourages teamwork. Those in two-parent families as well as those leading single-parent families are encouraged to find others who will help share the load. None of us were meant to parent our children by ourselves. In chapter six we'll suggest some ideas for building a community of support for your children and for yourself. In the meantime, know that you're not as alone as you may sometimes feel. God is with you always and you can trust him to provide all the help you'll need.

"I don't have the time." If this were a top ten list, this one would certainly be number one. There are so many demands on our time these days. Busyness is why we don't do all kinds of things we know we ought to be doing, like visiting relatives, getting enough rest, staying in shape, spending time with God, reading books, fixing the screen door, you name it. Busyness also keeps a lot of parents from being the spiritual leaders of their families. That's why the job so often gets outsourced to the church.

But as I've already said, with few exceptions no one has more time to spend with your children than you do. According to the experts, a church has about forty hours in a given year to influence the life of a child. Parents, on the other hand, have approximately *three thousand* hours in a year's time to influence a child.[3] Whether that's true or not depends on the family and the church, I suppose, but one thing we do know: all of us have the same twenty-four hours in each day, and the issue is not how much time we have but what we choose to do with it. All of us have plenty of time to devote to the things we believe are important.

Busyness also keeps a lot of parents from being the spiritual leaders of their families. That's why the job so often gets outsourced to the church.

We'll give some special attention to this topic in chapter three, but for now the question to ask is "How important is this to me?" If you truly believe that the spiritual welfare of your children is worth the time, you'll be able to find enough to get the job done. That's a guarantee. That's why we start here—acknowledging that God has commissioned us, and no one else, to take responsibility for passing faith on to our kids.

You'll never have all the time you would like, but let me say again that something is always better than nothing. Don't let a lack of time immobilize you or frustrate you to the point of doing nothing at all. If all you can do is spend one minute a day or one dinnertime a week talking with your children about God, by all means do it. God will bless that time in ways you can't even imagine.

"My children have disabilities or special needs." If you're the parent of a child with special needs, such as a learning or developmental disability, you may tend to shy away from trying to teach him or her very much about spiritual things. But even children who are unable to intellectually grasp the doctrines of the Christian faith can understand and learn a great deal about the love of God from their parents—much more than they can from anyone else. Special needs children may not always respond or behave as other children do, but they will be drawn to God when they experience God's love in the home.

Every child is, in a sense, a special needs child; each must be taught in a language that they can understand. Some children learn best by hearing, others by seeing, others by touch, and others by physical activity. We'll discuss how children learn in chapter five and suggest many ways that you can communicate God's love to your children regardless of their style of learning or special needs.

"My children go to a Christian school and attend church. They need a break from religion when they get home." It's unlikely that your kids need a break from "religion." What they need more of is to see their religious instruction validated and confirmed with Christlike lives at home. When kids experience a disconnect between what they're learning at church and what they're experiencing at home, they're not likely

---

❧ CROSS WALK ❧

Don't have the time? You need exercise, and like to take walks with your kids, right? Do this simple activity, which is great for children: take a walk around the neighborhood with your kids and see how many crosses you can find. You'll discover that they appear everywhere. Lines in the sidewalk, window panes, telephone poles—everywhere you look you'll see crosses. Take some pictures of them. Suggest to your children that whenever they see something that forms a cross, it's a good time to say a silent prayer of thanksgiving for what Jesus did for us on the cross.

to have a faith that is secure. The foundation of faith begins at home, and all other religious training is built upon that. You will have to decide how much religious instruction outside the home your children need. Total immersion in Christian culture can benefit many children, but it can have the opposite effect on others. One thing is sure: nothing can ever substitute for the kind of spiritual guidance, modeling, and unconditional love that parents are able to provide at home.

Remember that faith is less a matter of the head than it is of the heart. I've known kids in church youth groups and Christian schools who were model students, able to recite Scriptures, and name the twelve tribes of Israel—but they abandoned their faith once they left home and were no longer required by their parents to keep up the facade. They were never able to connect what they were learning intellectually about God with what they were feeling emotionally and experiencing at home. The love and grace of God can be extremely vague concepts unless the people in one's life are demonstrating them authentically and consistently. Christian education from the church and school is worthwhile, but it can never substitute for the relationship that can be provided by parents at home.

If your children are getting a great deal of Bible teaching and religious instruction outside the home, you may not need to add more at home. But you should never use this as an excuse to spend less time with your children having faith conversations and encouraging them in their walk with God. There are many ways to do that besides giving them more Bible lessons, as we'll see.

"I tried before but gave up on it." Maybe you gave up because your kids were complaining or you got busy or you forgot about it or you just decided it wasn't all that important. That's OK. Leading your children to walk with God involves a lot of stumbles and walking into walls. There aren't too many parents who say they had instant success when they started taking responsibility for their children's spiritual growth. Positive results often don't come right away. That's why it's important to make a commitment to lead your children in faith, taking into account the likelihood of failure and discouragement along the way.

Did you know that Thomas Edison, inventor of the light bulb, failed three hundred times to make a bulb that actually produced light? Most people would have given up after a hundred or so tries. But Edison had a vision for what he wanted to do and he kept going. Apparently, with each failure, he learned one more way *not* to make a light bulb.

What have you learned from your failures? Maybe a slight change of approach is needed. This book has been written to encourage you and to suggest some ideas that just might work for you and your family. As you try them, remember that failure is normal and to be expected. There is no right or perfect way to lead your children to faith, only your way, the way that works best for you. If you're willing to learn from your failures, your children will be willing to learn from you.

If you're willing to learn from your failures, your
children will be willing to learn from you.

"My kids aren't comfortable discussing spiritual things with me." Some children may feel uncomfortable discussing spiritual things with their parents simply because the children themselves lack knowledge. Others may feel uncomfortable because of their fear of being lectured or scolded. Others may feel uncomfortable because they believe they've outgrown it, much like they've outgrown Santa Claus or the Easter Bunny. I've also known children and teens who are uncomfortable discussing spiritual things simply because of a strained or broken relationship with their parents.

If your children seem reluctant to discuss spiritual things with you, the reasons probably have very little to do with God. They may just be bored or find spiritual things too abstract to understand. These are developmental rather than spiritual issues and can be remedied with a change in approach. We'll suggest ways to meet the developmental needs of your children later in this book.

It's also possible that you may be projecting onto your children your own discomfort with discussing spiritual things. Most children—younger ones at least—are naturally attracted to God and very interested in spiritual things. In the gospel of Mark, several children were brought to Jesus and the disciples attempted to shoo them away. But Jesus rebuked his disciples and said, "Let the little children come to me, and do not hinder them, for the kingdom of God belongs to such as these" (Mark 10:14). Then Jesus took the children in his arms, touched them, and blessed them. We don't know exactly what he did to bless them, but I can imagine a Jesus who laughed with them, played with them, and maybe even gave them lollipops.

All of us have blown it with our kids more times than we care to admit, but God forgives and heals and gives us the courage to move forward.

As parents we should take advantage of the natural sense of wonder and curiosity that children have about spiritual things. That's certainly one of the reasons why Jesus mentions (in what was recorded as the very next verse) that we should all become like little children—wide open to the things of God.

If the relationship you have with your children has become an obstacle for good communication, remember that God is in the healing business. We can't allow yesterday's failures or yesterday's sins to destroy what God wants to do in our lives or the lives of our children today. All of us have blown it with our kids more times than we care to admit, but God forgives and heals and gives us the courage to move forward.

"I'll start doing it . . . someday." No need for a lecture on procrastination here. We all know that someday is the one day in life that almost never gets here. Or when it does arrive, it shows up too late. I can tell you as a parent that when your kids are grown you will wonder where the time went. All of us who have raised children to adulthood now realize that we let too many "somedays" pass us by because we were waiting for more time or a better time.

Today is a good day to start leading your children to walk with God. They'll never be in a better place than they are right now—and neither will you. If you're waiting for the right moment or the right resources or the right opportunity, you'll probably be waiting forever. You don't need more knowledge than you have right now. You don't need more time that you have right now. You don't need more resources than you have right now. You have all you need to get started.

Begin with something as simple as prayer. Commit to praying for your children when you get up in the morning or when you go to bed at night. Or ask your children to pray for you. There is great power in prayer, and as you pray, God will provide you with the courage and resources you need to become the answer to your own prayers.

You don't need more knowledge than you have right now. You don't need more time that you have right now. You don't need more resources than you have right now. You have all you need to get started.

"My kids seem to be doing fine so far." That's great. Chances are good that they really are doing quite well spiritually. But it's doubtful that they are doing well by accident. You've had a lot to do with that and there's certainly more that you can continue to do.

I can tell you from experience that sometimes what you see on the outside can hide a great deal of what's happening on the inside. Unless you're having regular faith conversations with your children and expressing God's love and faithfulness to them at home, you may never know what your children are actually learning about God.

Jenny is a good example of this. For many years, Rick and Dana assumed that she was getting all she needed from her Sunday school classes and later on from her youth group. On the outside, she seemed fine, actively participating in church activities and never giving her parents any real trouble. But on the inside, Jenny was hiding deep feelings of resentment and insecurity that were chipping away at her very unstable foundation of faith.

Like the proverbial squeaky wheel that gets the grease, many parents make the mistake of waiting for their children to misbehave or reject their faith before getting involved. Don't do that. If your children are doing fine so far, be thankful, but commit yourself now to become even more engaged in their continued spiritual growth. Make sure that they're getting all they need to develop a healthy relationship with God, to become lovers and followers of Christ, and to be part of a strong faith community. Unless you know what's going on in your child's spiritual life, there's nothing you can do to help meet his or her spiritual needs.

"My kids are teenagers or young adults. It's too late."

Regret and disappointment come easily to parents whose children have become teenagers. They're rarely prepared for the normal changes that take place in their adolescent children and often misinterpret much of their behavior. For example, when teenagers no longer want to participate in activities like family devotions or family traditions, parents are likely to interpret this as *rebellion*. When teenagers no longer want to spend as much time with them as with their friends, parents are likely to interpret this as *rejection*. But neither of these things are true. The vast majority of teenagers still want a good relationship with their parents and actually are happier with them than when they're with their friends.[4]

It's important to remember that teenagers are at a crucial time for faith development. As children they learned a lot about *your* faith; now they need to learn about *their* faith. They no longer want to believe what you believe; they want to make it their own. As parents, we shouldn't be discouraged when teenagers appear to be rejecting their faith. More often than not, they're simply setting aside their childhood faith in favor of one that is more real to them, more personal. It's very important for parents to encourage their children in this process and remain engaged and available as they learn to walk with God on their own.

❧ FAITH CONVERSATION BOX ❧

Looking for simple ways to start faith conversations? Here's one, and you never have to leave the dinner table. Fill a box or jar with questions like the ones below. At dinnertime, have your kids pull one out for discussion. Everyone has to give a response.

Who is your favorite Bible character?

What is a fun memory you have of Sunday school?

What do you think Heaven will be like?

What did you do today to make God smile?

How does God want you to treat people who are mean to you?

What skill do you have that God can use?

What question would you like to ask God?

What do you think God looks like?

What one thing about our world would you like God to change? How can you help?

What's your favorite Bible verse?

What's the most fun you've had helping others?

Describe the funniest thing that ever happened when you were at church.

How could you introduce a friend to Jesus?

What, in your opinion, is the best ministry in our church?

If your faith were a color, what color would it be?

Describe something that happened to you that was an answer to prayer.

What are some things, or people—besides God—that people worship?

Talk about something you could do to help the poor.

And more that you come up with!

But perhaps you have children who are older now and are far from a relationship with God. Maybe they've made some bad choices and resist any attempt you make to reconnect with them or to encourage them in their faith. This can be very painful. Just remember that God is well acquainted with your grief. *All* of his children have gone astray (Romans 3:23), yet he never gives up on any of us. When Jesus wanted the perfect description of God as a loving Father, he told a story of a son who had rebelled and turned his back on his family heritage (Luke 15:11-32). What makes this story so remarkable is not the son's decision to repent and return home, but the father's patience and willingness to forgive his son after all that he had done.

Too late can be a quite depressing thought when it comes to our children. So here's my advice: you don't want to go there at all. *It's never too late.* Remember that where there is life, there is hope. In fact, even in death, there is hope. We never know what thoughts, prayers, and actions a person takes to the grave—whether they did, or did not, choose to obey Christ. If one of your children is far from God right now, rest assured that God has not given up on him or her. He isn't finished with your children, nor is he finished with you. How many people do you know who have come back to the faith of their parents in middle age or even later? Many do! There is always hope, and we should never stop doing the things that we know will have a positive impact on the spiritual lives of our children, no matter how old they, or we, are.

the first commission

God's commission to parents has not changed since it was first given to us in Deuteronomy 6. And it wasn't overridden by the Great Commission of Jesus in Matthew 28, in which he commands all followers to "go and make disciples of all nations." The Great Commission has, of course, provided the motive as well as the motivation for every evangelistic effort and missionary endeavor since the day Jesus spoke those words.

But it's important to remember the Great Commission does not cancel out the First Commission that was given to parents in Deuteronomy 6. In fact, the Great Commission assumes the First Commission—that parents would be making disciples in their own homes. But it can't stop there, Jesus says. The gospel, or good news of Christ, is not just for our families and our own kind—it's for the whole world. That's what was revolutionary about the gospel; this news was to be taken to the ends of the earth.

Our Lord would agree that a Christian's first responsibility (if he or she is a parent) is to instruct his or her children in the faith and to disciple them to become Christ-followers. I once heard a wise pastor ask this question, based on Mark 8:36: "What does it profit a man to reach the whole world for Christ, yet lose his own children?" It's a valid question—one that's led to a good deal of regret for some evangelists I know. While it's essential for us to take the good news of Christ to the world, Jesus doesn't require us to sacrifice our own children to do it. Our Father in Heaven has already sacrificed his own.

1 || Spend some time thinking about your personal spiritual journey. How did you come to faith in Christ?

2 || What do these Scriptures tell us about God's plan for passing the faith from one generation to the next?

Deuteronomy 6:5-7

Psalms 78:4-6

Ephesians 6:4

3 || Who or what do you think influences your children the most? Rank the list below:

___ Peers (same-age friends)
___ Parents
___ Popular culture (media, music, TV, celebrities)
___ Other adults (teachers, pastors, other mentors)
___ Grandparents (or other extended family)
___ Other: _____

4 || Which of the following "barriers" have discouraged you from being more involved in the spiritual lives of your children?

❑ Lack of experience: "I just don't know where to begin."
❑ Lack of confidence: "I'm not spiritual enough."
❑ Lack of energy: "I'm too tired at the end of the day."
❑ Lack of family harmony: "Our family is a mess."
❑ Lack of time: "We're too busy."
❑ Lack of consistency: "I tried before but gave up on it."
❑ Lack of a relationship: "My kids aren't comfortable discussing spiritual things with me."
❑ Lack of urgency: "I'll start doing it . . . someday."
❑ Lack of motivation: "My kids seem to be doing fine so far."
❑ Lack of knowledge: "I never realized I was supposed to do it."
❑ Lack of responsibility: "We take them to church. That should be enough."
❑ Other: _____

5 || What are some things you're currently doing in your home to pass faith on to your children? (We're just getting started, so don't be discouraged no matter the answer here.)

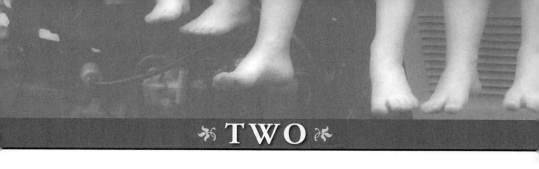

commitment

I guess turnabout is fair play.

When my son Nathan was still at home, I would often drag him off to conferences where I was a speaker and use him as an example in my talks. After embarrassing him on many occasions, I finally realized that it was not such a good idea to use your children as sermon illustrations (or book illustrations either, for that matter) unless you ask their permission ahead of time.

But recently I went to a conference where Nathan was the speaker, not me. During his talk he called me up on stage and used me as a prop for a little object lesson. "Just look at him," Nathan grinned to the audience while pointing at me. "I don't know how it happened, but somehow my dad turned out just like me."

We do look alike in some ways. Actually, Nate takes after his mother and is much better looking than me. But we do share the same hairline (or lack of one), we both have bad eyesight and wear glasses and, on that particular day, we were even dressed alike. Now *that* was embarrassing for both of us.

Nate pointed out that he has picked up a lot of my mannerisms. For example, I often greet people by saying "Howdy." I don't know why I do this, but I do. I never realized this, but Nate admitted he does the same thing despite his many attempts to stop sounding like his hillbilly father.

Like it or not, we all become a lot like our parents. Unless your children were adopted, they've probably inherited many of your physical characteristics—skin color, hair color, size, weight, and facial features. They also may have inherited your athletic abilities (or lack of), your intellectual abilities, your personality traits, or your artistic and musical abilities.

You will pass on a variety of unique traits and characteristics to your children, some of which, no doubt, you never intended to pass on to them at all.

If you've adopted children, they will likely pick up many of your family characteristics by virtue of the fact that they live in the same house with you. Our youngest son, Corey, was born in South Korea. He doesn't look anything like me or my wife or any of our natural born children, yet in most other ways he's a chip off the old block. He spoke fluent Korean and had a completely different worldview when we adopted him at age five, but today he sounds exactly like us and has many of our same family likes, dislikes, traits, and mannerisms. No matter how hard we tried to help him hang on to some of his Korean-ness (if I may coin a phrase), he—just like our other kids—grew up to become an all-American boy and a full-fledged member of the Rice family.

This is natural and more or less inevitable. You will pass on a variety of unique traits and characteristics to your children, some of which, no doubt, you never intended to pass on to them at all.

But here's the point: faith is *not* passed on that way. There are no guarantees—at all—that your children will adopt your faith simply by virtue of the fact that you gave them their DNA or that they grew up in the same house with you. That's because faith is an individual choice that each and every person must make on his or her own. No one is automatically born into the

family of God when they are born (or adopted) into a Christian fam
must be born a second time (John 3:3) and adopted by God into h.... ....y
(Ephesians 1:5).

That's why we have to make a firm commitment to raise up our children in the faith and give them every opportunity to make it their own. It's not enough to simply *know* that God has commissioned us to do this. We also have to commit ourselves to making sure our children get the instruction and encouragement they need every day to make Christ their Savior and to choose to follow him for the rest of their lives.

The fact that they were the children and grandchildren of Abraham and Isaac and Moses wasn't enough. They had short memories and wandering eyes.

joshua's commitment

In the Old Testament book of Joshua, we read the story of God's people, the Israelites, who had been in slavery for three hundred years and wandered in the desert for another forty. But with the help of God and under the leadership of Joshua, they finally reached the promised land. Along the way, God gave the Israelites impressive victories in what may have been as many as thirty or more battles without suffering a single defeat (see Joshua 12). Walls unexplainably fell down, rivers stopped flowing, and even the sun stood still for a day's time. You would have thought the Israelites would never turn their back on the God who had miraculously delivered them out of slavery and given them their land, their protection, and their prosperity.

But that wasn't the case. At the end of the book of Joshua we find the Israelites chasing after false gods. The mere fact that they were the children and grandchildren of Abraham and Isaac and Moses wasn't enough. They had short memories and wandering eyes. So Joshua delivered a stirring challenge to his generation, one that continues to resonate with us today.

> *"So now: Fear GOD. Worship him in total commitment. Get rid of the gods your ancestors worshiped on the far side of The River (The Euphrates) and in Egypt. You, worship GOD.*
>
> *If you decide that it's a bad thing to worship GOD, then choose a god you'd rather serve—and do it today. Choose one of the gods your ancestors worshiped from the country beyond The River, or one of the gods of the Amorites, on whose land you're now living. As for me and my family, we will worship GOD." (Joshua 24:14, 15, The Message)*

Several things come to mind when I read this account from the Bible. First, the influence we have on our children and grandchildren can be negative as well as positive. Even though the Israelites had witnessed the power of God, they remembered that their ancestors had worshiped idols (remember the golden calf?). Some of those idols were apparently looking pretty good to Joshua's generation.

Second, there will always be other gods to choose from. We should never make the mistake of thinking that our children will naturally serve the God of the Bible. By nature our default setting—and our children's—is to follow false gods.[5] If we don't commit ourselves to leading and teaching our children to follow Christ, they probably won't.

Third, while the pagan gods of Joshua's day were made of silver and gold, the gods that entice us and our children today are no less attractive. We're seduced every day by the god of secularism, the god of narcissism, the god of hedonism, the god of materialism, the god of popularity, the god of fame, the god of power, the god of sex. All of these gods offer us and our children tempting alternatives to the God who sent his Son to die for our sins.

Joshua knew there were other gods he could serve, but he chose to love and serve the only one deserving of his worship—the God of Abraham and Isaac and Moses—and he was determined that his family would do the same. The only way we can pass faith from one generation to the next is to do it with the same kind of courage and commitment that Joshua did.

FAMILY DEVOTIONS

FAMILY TRADITIONS

❧ RAISE AN EBENEZER ❧

In 1 Samuel 7:12, 13, Samuel set up a stone monument called an Ebenezer, which means "Stone of Help." The monument would commemorate how God helped the Israelites win a victory over the Philistines. It remained there as a permanent marker so that the people would never forget what God had done.

Has God blessed your family in a special way? You may not be able to build a stone monument like Samuel, but you might be able to create something that will last for years as a testimony to God's blessing and to your commitment to love and serve him. A scrapbook, a wall hanging, or sculpture on display in your home can become a modern-day Ebenezer to constantly remind your family, and anyone else who sees it, what God has done.

Or find a few smooth, rounded stones from a nearby creek bed, your yard, or your garden. Have each family member paint their name on their stone along with, perhaps, a simple picture representing how God has helped that family member. Kids will love this one, and the stones can remain inside your home for years.

Other ways you can set up Ebenezers? There are as many as you can come up with. In 2001 my wife Marci was diagnosed with a brain tumor. Her amazing recovery from surgery was an incredible gift from God to us, and I shared her story with friends and relatives on a web page: www.waynerice.com/marci.htm. We've left it there for quite a few years now as a kind of Ebenezer for our family, maybe not as permanent as a stone marker, but one that continues to encourage us when we return to it. The page blesses others who get the opportunity to read it as well.

---

a personal commitment

Joshua's commitment began with himself. Certainly one of the most important principles of leadership is that you must lead by example. Joshua was first in line to accept the terms of his own challenge: "As for me and my family, we will worship GOD." If we want our children to live godly lives, our commitment has to begin with "me."

I think of this every time I get on a plane. Instructions are almost always given by the flight attendant on the use of the oxygen mask. *"Should there be a change in cabin pressure, an oxygen mask will drop from the compartment above your head. . . . Pull the mask toward you to start the oxygen flow . . ."* Those instructions usually continue with words that seem to violate our natural parental instincts. *"Put your oxygen mask on first,* then *assist your child."*

The principle is clear and applicable to raising children in the faith. You can't really pass on to your children something that you yourself don't have.

I was privileged to grow up in a Christian home. My dad was a building contractor and my mother a full-time mom. But more importantly, they were both unabashed lovers of God. Nothing was more important to them than being in church every Sunday (morning and evening) and any other day of the week the church had services, which was quite often. I have all kinds of wonderful family memories, but without question the most enduring of these are memories of my parents praising God, singing hymns and gospel songs, or standing up in church with tears streaming down their faces as they shared what God was doing in their lives. Reading the Bible, praying together, and talking about spiritual things was so natural in our house that I couldn't imagine families living any other way. My parents weren't perfect— we all knew that—but I never doubted the authenticity of their faith in God or their complete devotion to Christ. They not only talked about it, they lived it. It was their example that laid the tracks for my own life.

The principle is clear and applicable to raising children in the faith. You can't really pass on to your children something that you yourself don't have.

There really is no better way than this to teach your children to put God first in their lives. If you are doing all you can to stay close to God, your kids will be much more likely to want to do the same. It's important to remember this, because we can't force our kids to become Christians. We have no control over what they choose to believe or not believe. But you do have control over *you*—and what you do will more than likely become the pattern that your kids will follow.

I have a good friend whose name is Dan. Like me, he's an avid fisherman. Unlike me, he has a really nice fishing boat and takes every opportunity he can to get out on the water. Sometimes I go fishing with him. He excitedly called me on a recent Saturday afternoon to tell me that the albacore tuna were biting offshore. "I'm going out after them tomorrow morning," he said. "Wanna go?"

If you are doing all you can to stay close to God, your kids will be much more likely to want to do the same.

You bet I did. But there was one problem. "Tomorrow is Sunday," I reminded Dan. "What about church?"

"We can go to church any Sunday, but the albacore are only going to be around for a few days," he said. "We can get tapes of the pastor's sermon."

I had to turn him down. I can't remember a Sunday in my whole life when my father wasn't in church—and he was a busy man with a successful contracting business. He'd often have to work late into the night to get things done, but he never missed church. He also had hobbies and loved to go camping and fishing. But never on Sunday. That was a lesson I learned well, and I've tried to teach it to my own kids.

"Dan," I said, "I hope you catch a lot of fish. But I also hope you understand that you might be sending your daughter a message you may not want to send—that fishing is more important to you than worshiping God. I know that's not true, but kids don't always get that. Tell me, what are you going to say when she wants to go to the beach with her friends on a Sunday?"

I don't want to sound legalistic or self-righteous here. There certainly have been times when I've had to miss church for one reason or another (and not all of those reasons were noble ones). My point is simply that the only way a parent can ever hope to teach children to love God with all of their heart and soul and mind is for that truth to emerge from what the parent has in his or her own heart and soul and mind. Only then can the lessons that come up at the table, at bedtime, on walks, in the busyness of the day, or the first thing in the morning, have any credibility at all. Only when parents inwardly and outwardly love God and put him first in their lives will children get the message, from the moment they walk through the doorposts of their house, that God is sovereign and worthy of our love and obedience.

Many years ago, I was hurriedly leaving home to speak at a parent seminar. As I was leaving, I noticed one of my tools had been left out in the driveway to rust. I dashed into the house and chewed out my son for being irresponsible. I angrily told him to either start putting my tools back where they belonged or stop using them altogether! He tried defending himself, but I reduced him to tears before I sped off in my car so that I could teach parents how to keep the relationship with their kids in good shape. The irony of that incident really didn't hit me until halfway through my seminar when I realized that I had completely blown it with my own son. When I got home I had to ask his forgiveness, which became a powerful moment of healing between us.

If we want to raise children who love and serve God, we will love and serve God ourselves. Children don't always hear what we say, but they watch what we *do*. And as Scripture teaches us, what we do is always the true proof of the pudding (Matthew 7:21-27; James 1:22). What we say to our children about faith won't mean much to them unless they observe us putting faith into practice in our daily lives. We can't get our kids to become something we are not.

a shared commitment

Joshua's commitment also included members of his family. *As for me and my family, we will serve God.* In those days and in that culture, it was possible for heads of households to make such declarations on behalf of their families, which included wives, children, extended family, servants, and anyone else connected with the family. Some historians estimate that Old Testament families typically averaged as many as sixty people. It would be wrong to suggest here that Joshua was making a faith commitment for all of them. But we can be sure that he was declaring his intent to serve God himself and to lead his entire family to do the same.

Anyone can make that same kind of family commitment today, but—if you are married—it has to begin with a commitment to and *with* your spouse. Both of you—husband and wife—must be committed to establishing a Christian home for your children and to keeping your marriage strong.

Marci and I have always tried to make a big deal out of our wedding anniversary. We put it on the family calendar and start making plans weeks if not months ahead of time. Our kids always knew it was coming up. When they were children, we would sometimes do something special together as a family to celebrate that anniversary. One year we took them all out of school for the day and went to Disneyland. We wanted them to understand how special our marriage (and our family) was and celebrating with something they enjoyed (as well as with us) communicated that very effectively. On other anniversaries, we left our children at home with a sitter and went away for a weekend trip to a romantic getaway, which also communicated volumes to our kids. They knew that we were away being romantic, having fun, and doing what lovers do. That can be a very reassuring thing for children. Some kids (especially teenagers) can't imagine their parents doing anything like that.

More importantly, when couples give their wedding anniversaries a high priority, it's more often than not an indicator of the vitality of their marriage. People just don't celebrate things that are unhealthy, dying, or already dead.

I've always believed that one of the best gifts you can give your kids is a strong marriage. If you want your children to feel secure and have a solid foundation upon which they can build their own faith and values, then it makes a lot of sense to protect and nurture the relationship you have with your spouse. Don't allow your career, your house, your kids, or anything else to destroy the love you have for each other. Teenagers, especially, need to see that mom and dad have something special going. When they see you and your spouse touching each other, kissing each other, saying nice things to each other, and treating each other with love and respect, they'll feel more loved themselves. When children can see the love between their parents, they'll know that there is plenty of love available for them. In addition, a healthy marriage can become an important model for your children of the love and faithfulness of God. The Bible makes this comparison frequently. So should we.

> **⅋ ANNIVERSARY FAMILY DAYS ⅋**
>
> While there's nothing wrong with a romantic evening out on your anniversary (without the kids), why not also plan a celebration for the family as well? Maybe do a bigger trip every other year and a smaller one on the other years. Take the kids to an amusement park or do a weekend outing at a fancy hotel or just go out to dinner together. If your children look forward to your anniversary each year, it will not only teach them the importance of marriage but also provide them with the security of knowing that your marriage is strong and worth celebrating.

Having said all this, let me again offer a word of encouragement to single parents. Two parents are not required to raise godly children. While the biblical norm is for both mother and father to be fully engaged with their children as parents, we know that God is a "father to the fatherless" (Psalm 68:5) and the provider of help and comfort for both single moms and single dads (Isaiah 40:25-31). While I've never been a single parent, I'm well aware of how difficult it can be to parent alone. You face unique pressures and challenges that two-parent families are most often spared, but I'm also confident that God can provide you with all that you need to be successful as a parent.

That's why he created the church (which we'll discuss more in chapter six). Rest assured that being single does not automatically disqualify you or anyone else from raising children who will love and serve God.

a long-range commitment

Two fathers greeted each other in the village square one day; each was accompanied by his son. "Moshe, my friend. I want you meet my son Reuben, the lawyer." To which Moshe replied, "What a fine son, Mordecai! And I would like to introduce you to my son Bennie, the doctor." Each boy was ten years old.

Two fathers bragging about their sons? Perhaps. But Moshe and Mordecai come from a long line of Jewish fathers who set their children on life trajectories that often came to pass. Isaac prophesied that his son Jacob would become a strong leader and Jacob prophesied about his children and grandchildren as well.[6] We may not be able to make prophesies like that about our children, but we can have high aspirations for them and help them to see themselves as we see them and as God sees them.

When children can see the love between their parents, they'll know that there is plenty of love available for them. In addition, a healthy marriage can become an important model for your children of the love and faithfulness of God.

I've always been fascinated by Solomon's description of children as "arrows in the hands of a warrior" (Psalm 127:4, 5). While I'm not an archer myself, I think it's safe to say that when warriors shoot their arrows, they usually have a clear target in view. You don't just fling arrows into the air and hope they hit something somewhere.

When Joshua proclaimed, "As for me and my family, we will worship God," he had a target in view. He had a vision not only for himself but also for his entire household.

What do you want your children to become when they grow up? Do you have a target in mind, a goal or a vision for your children that will inform and guide your efforts as a parent? As the saying goes: If you aim at nothing, that's what you'll hit every time. I'm amazed sometimes how many parents haven't really thought about what they want their children to become and what it will take to help them realize that goal. They just prefer to leave it all up to chance, good (or bad) fortune, or to the children themselves.

You may not be able to control all that your child does, but you can most certainly control what you *do. That's the purpose for setting goals for your kids.*

Raising children in the faith is not like that. Any commitment to raising godly children is a commitment to long-range parenting. The goal of a Christian parent is not just to have a house full of obedient and well-behaved children. It's not about getting through the day or the week. It's about raising capable, self-reliant adults who will love and serve God after they leave home.

It's clear from Scripture that God has a long-term perspective for our kids. We may not be able to see the big picture, the finished product, but God can. Even while your kids were in the womb, God had big plans for them (see Isaiah 49:5; Jeremiah 1:5). Did you? Maybe not. We don't usually think that far ahead. When a baby is born, the doctor doesn't announce, "Congratulations, you've just given birth to a future Nobel Prize winner." That might be nice to hear, but really all we initially care about is whether our baby is born in good health.

At some point, however, it's important to set our eyes on the prize, as the old saying goes. Have you thought about your goal as a parent? Goal setting is a universally accepted principle of effective leadership that certainly has an application to parenting.

Dream a little for your son or daughter. What kind of person do you want him or her to become? Obviously, you can't predict how your kids are going to turn out because every person is an individual who must ultimately decide for themselves what they want to be and do. Still, as a parent, you can set some goals for your kids that will not only be a kind of road map for their lives but also help you as a parent to guide and encourage your kids along that path. You may not be able to control all that your child does, but you can most certainly control what *you* do. That's the purpose for setting goals for your kids. Parents play a huge role in the development of children and those who understand that from the beginning will be in the best position to see their hopes and dreams for their kids become a reality.

Let's break this area down a little bit more.

A worthy goal for your kids? Let me suggest Luke 2:52.
In this verse, we're given a summary glimpse into the childhood and adolescence of Jesus: "And Jesus grew in wisdom and in stature, and in favor with God and men." From this verse we see that Jesus matured in every area of his life—the intellectual (wisdom), the physical (stature), the spiritual (in favor with God), and the social (in favor with men). Isn't this how you would like your son or daughter to grow up? When my kids were young, I often substituted the names of my own children in that verse as a kind of prayer for them: "And (Nathan/Amber/Corey) grew in wisdom and stature, and in favor with God and men." Isn't that something you would like for your children? That verse is very attainable for children who have loving, committed parents. Jesus was first a baby, then a child, then a teenager just like your kids are or will be. He was *fully human*, as the Apostles' Creed puts it, and we are encouraged as his followers to imitate him.

How did Jesus grow to excel in all of these areas? The gospels don't give us too many details about Jesus' adolescence, but we do get a clue in verse 51: "Then he [Jesus] went down to Nazareth with them [his parents] and *was obedient to them*" (emphasis added). Mary and Joseph were obviously very good parents. It always blows me away to try to imagine setting limits and providing discipline for the Son of God! But they did what every good parent must do—they were actively involved in raising their young son to manhood. They had a vision of what he would someday become and they never stopped believing in him. God trusted Mary and Joseph with his only Son.

And God has trusted you with your kids. They are his, but he has given you the responsibility to help them become what he created them to be. While you can't control every aspect or outcome of your son's or daughter's lives, you can provide appropriate amounts of encouragement and influence. While there are no guarantees or magic formulas for raising godly kids, your efforts to be a good parent will pay off.

If you want to get a little more specific regarding your parenting goals, you might find it worthwhile to sit down and write something like the "sample parenting goal" shown on the next page. Again, dream a bit for your son or daughter. What qualities of character do you believe are important? What kind of person do you want him or her to become? Write these things down and commit yourself to doing all you can to encourage and inspire your son or daughter in those areas. Use what you've written as a reminder to hang in there, even when things aren't going so smoothly. But a word of warning: Do not use this list as a reminder to yourself—or your kids—of how far they still have to go. That will only frustrate everybody. But if you do have a mental picture of the kind of person you want your kids to become, and treat them accordingly, there's a good chance they will live up to your expectations of them.

The power of words—for good and bad. Years ago I heard a young woman named Cheryl Prewitt share a story from her childhood. When she was only four years old, she spent many hours at her father's small country grocery store. Almost daily, the milkman would come into the store with his delivery and greet her with the words, "Good morning, Cheryl. How's my little Miss America?" At first she giggled when he called her that—but over time, she grew comfortable with it, even started to like it a little. Soon the milkman's greeting became a childhood fantasy, then a teenage dream, then a young woman's challenge. In 1980, she walked a runway stage in Atlantic City as the newly crowned Miss America.

> **A SAMPLE PARENTING GOAL**
>
> We, the parents of Kyle Jeffrey Meadows, pledge ourselves to help him grow up to become a capable, independent, and godly man, who will . . .
>
> - be able to make wise decisions based on sound principles
> - be emotionally and spiritually strong
> - enter into healthy relationships with other people
> - be able to accept responsibility for himself, his family, and his vocation
> - be able to overcome difficult times with perseverance and grace
> - if he marries, be a faithful and loving husband and parent
> - glorify God in his work and his service to others

Hearing that story reminded me of how powerful our words of encouragement to children can be. I've learned that some of the words I've said to teenagers who were in my youth groups, like "I think you would make a great youth pastor someday," can be life-changing. Sometimes all we need to do is put an idea into the heads of youngsters to help them see themselves in a completely new way.

Sadly, the reverse is also true. Quite a few years ago I wrote in one of my other books about the "myth of the teenage werewolf," a negative stereotype about teenagers that can paralyze parents and become a self-fulfilling prophecy.[7] Recent studies confirm that this continues to be true. "When parents expect their teenagers to conform to negative stereotypes, those teenagers are in fact more likely to do so."[8] When parents fail to believe in their kids—or believe the worst about them—their kids also fail to believe in themselves.

But parents who believe in their children and have a positive outlook for their children's future are much more likely to raise children who believe in themselves and pursue it for themselves.

Training them for the long term—in the way they should go. Every child must choose his or her own path, of course, but the Bible tells us that if we point our children in the right direction, there is a strong likelihood they'll keep going that way. That's the message of Proverbs 22:6: "Train a child in the way he should go, and when he is old he will not turn from it." That's a very hopeful and encouraging verse, but it's important to remember that this is a proverb, not a promise. It wasn't meant to be a magic formula or a burden on parents. The book of Proverbs gives us principles to live by, not laws to obey.

Sometimes all we need to do is put an idea into the heads of youngsters to help them see themselves in a completely new way.

It's also helpful to remember that the word *train* in this passage comes not from the worlds of education or psychology but from the world of agriculture. Gardeners *train* their vines along their natural bent, or patterns of growth, so that they will become as beautiful and fruitful as God intended them to be. We must never try to force our kids to become something they are not. We all know parents who have made the mistake of trying to live their lives vicariously through their kids. You want to stay as far away from that extreme as possible. Setting goals and having high hopes for our kids is not about us; it's about giving our children the guidance and confidence they need to become what God created them to be.

I've known fathers who pushed their sons to excel in sports such as football and basketball when those sons had little interest in sports or lacked the athletic ability to compete. They were more likely to win a chess tournament or first prize at the science fair—which would have been great things had they been allowed to do so. This kind of pressure can frustrate children and cause them to fail in life. Wise parents allow their children to pursue their natural bent and to succeed in areas where they've been gifted by God. If they can succeed in those areas, they'll be more likely to succeed in other areas of life as well.

For as long as I can remember, I've loved to doodle. I remember as a child sitting in church with my parents, drawing cartoons and designs on the church bulletin to pass the time during a dull sermon. In those days, doodling in church was considered bad behavior, like chewing gum or throwing paper airplanes. But my father never scolded me. Instead, he just gave me more paper. His vision for me was bigger than simply raising a well-behaved churchgoer. It included my development as a creative artist. He saw the big picture, the long-range goal. I didn't become the architect that my father thought I would eventually become, but my artistic skills have been put to use in lots of other ways.

a practical commitment

Commitments aren't much good unless you act on them. If you've made the commitment to become the spiritual leader or coleader of your home, that's wonderful. But the next question to ask is: What are you going to do? A fundamental principle of leadership is that if you don't act on a decision within four days of making it, there is a 90 percent chance that the decision will never be acted on at all.

How will you put your commitment into action? What changes will you make? What do you plan to do?

Before we go much further, let me say that you don't need to make big changes all at once. Sailors know this truth: if you try to turn a ship too sharply, you'll capsize the boat. The best way to make changes in your family life is to do it one step at a time. You might begin simply by committing to a daily time of prayer with your spouse (perhaps just before you go to bed at night) to ask for God's help and direction as you try to lead your children to love and serve him. That's a great start that will reap huge dividends. It will not only tap into the blessings of God for your family but also keep your commitment and mission as a parent in full view every day.

On the other hand, if you're a person who likes charts and spreadsheets, let me suggest that you sit down with your spouse and create a customized plan for your family's spiritual growth that includes various activities that you commit to on a daily, weekly, monthly, or annual basis. You can start with something similar to this:

A PLAN FOR OUR FAMILY'S SPIRITUAL GROWTH				
	DAILY	WEEKLY	MONTHLY	ANNUALLY
What we have been doing	Have dinner together as a family Pray before meals	Attend church together as a family		Family vacation (two weeks) Celebrate birthdays, wedding anniversaries, holidays together as a family
What we will begin to do immediately	Pray together for our kids every day Have regular faith conversations around the dinner table	Make Saturdays a nonnegotiable family day Watch a favorite TV show together as a family, and talk about it afterwards	Encourage kids to attend children/youth activities at church Watch a Christian movie with our kids	Incorporate into our vacation something that involves mission and service
What we will consider doing in the future	Give our kids a blessing each day as they leave for school	Have a weekly fun night Regular family devotionals Read bedtime stories to our children	Do a family service project Take a day off from work to spend with our kids	Celebrate our children's spiritual birthdays

You're finding lots of ideas in this book to choose from, and let me stress again that you should not try to do them all right away. I'm a believer in the old adage "something is always better than nothing." None of us can do everything, but all of us can do *something*. Just find the "something" that seems most important for you and put it into action—even if it's a baby step. A commitment without action is no commitment at all.

a public commitment

Have you ever made a commitment and then never told anyone about it? How long did that commitment last?

Not long ago I made a commitment to lose about thirty pounds so that I could get back into the left side of my closet, where I banish the clothes that no longer fit me. They've been hanging there for years. It took several months, but the low-carb diet I chose this time actually worked, and I lost the weight. Now that I'm wearing all those old clothes again, people comment that I'm thinner . . . but hopelessly out of style.

Was it the diet that caused me to lose weight? Actually, no. I've tried that diet before and have discovered that it can actually cause you to eat and gain more, not less. What caused me to lose weight this time was that I decided to go public with it so that people around me could hold me accountable. I made sure everyone I knew was put on notice that I was on a diet, as in, "Please don't tempt me!" I carried little placards that I set on the church's doughnut table: UNDER PENALTY OF LAW—DO NOT OFFER ONE OF THESE TO WAYNE! My family and friends knew that I no longer did ice cream, cookies, French fries, fondue, or fettuccine alfredo. I've discovered that only when I have the support and cooperation of the family and friends around me can I possibly hope to have success reaching my personal goals.

The same is true with any commitments we make to God. When Joshua challenged the Israelites to choose which god they would serve, he not only set an example by choosing to serve God himself but by going public with the choice he had made. He boldly announced his intention to serve God as a way of holding himself and his family accountable to all who were within the sound of his voice. No one had to guess or make assumptions about what Joshua and his family's choice was going to be.

Marriage is a good example of a public commitment. One of the reasons we go to all the trouble to file legal documents and hold expensive wedding ceremonies in the presence of God, the state, the church, family, and friends is not because it's required but because a public commitment to faithfulness in marriage provides couples with the accountability needed for success. When people ask me the secret to longevity in marriage, I sometimes tell them that Marci and I are as committed to marriage as we are to each other. I love my wife, but there were times early in our forty-four years of marriage when mere *feelings* of love were simply not strong enough to keep us together. But our vows were. The truth and commitment of our marriage vows have kept us faithful to each other when the feelings could not—and for that we are grateful.

When people ask me the secret to longevity in marriage, I sometimes tell them that Marci and I are as committed to marriage as we are to each other.

I always enjoy attending church services when parents bring their children forward for infant baptism, christening, or a baby dedication ceremony. Regardless of your beliefs about what happens to the child during these ceremonies (which may or may not include water baptism), the focus of the service is not so much on the child's commitment; it's really about the commitment of the parents. In front of the entire congregation, parents make a promise to God to train up their child in the way that he or she should go and to raise them in the "nurture and admonition of the Lord" (Ephesians 6:4, *KJV*). Sometimes other family members stand in solidarity with them, and the entire congregation pledges to encourage the parents and hold them accountable and pray for them.

Of course, these ceremonies don't guarantee that a child will grow up to follow Christ and come to have faith on his or her own. But when parents make a public commitment to raise their children in the Lord, there is motivating power in that proclamation. Every time I attend a wedding today, I'm reminded of the vows I made to my wife so long ago. Every time I attend a baby dedication ceremony, I'm also reminded of the promises I made to pass my faith on to my children.

Just as Joshua went public with his commitment, so should we. You may not need a formal ceremony to declare your intent to raise up children in the Lord, but don't rule that out as a possibility. You might find it meaningful to conduct a special service of commitment and blessing for your home similar to the one shown on the next page. Send out invitations to friends and neighbors and ask them to join you and your family as you dedicate your home and your family to God.

When God commanded parents to "tie them [the commandments] as symbols on your hands and bind them on your foreheads. Write them on the doorframes of your houses and on your gates" (Deuteronomy 6:8, 9), there was implied in that command a public proclamation of faith. We may not need to put neon signs in our windows or loudspeakers in the front yard, but we certainly can take every opportunity to let our children and those who care about us know where we stand. *"As for me and my family, we will worship God."*

❧ A SERVICE OF DEDICATION AND BLESSING FOR YOUR HOME ❧

Here's an outline for a simple service that begins outside your home and then moves through each room of the house.[9] (For this reason, you probably don't want more people to attend than your house can comfortably hold.) Adapt this service to your unique home. A service like this would especially be appropriate upon moving into a new home.

Invite friends, neighbors, family members, your pastor, and other church leaders. The pastor can lead the service or you can do it yourself. Involve some of your guests—and especially your children—by allowing them to read some of the Scripture passages or to pray at each stop along the way.

Gather in the driveway, on the front lawn, or in the garage. Begin by explaining why you are conducting this service. Read Joshua 24:14, 15. Say something like, "Thank you for joining with us today as we dedicate our home and our lives together as a family to the Lord. Just as Joshua declared, 'As for me and my family, we will worship God,' so we want to publicly declare our intent to make our home a Christian home in every way."

Move to the front door. Read Revelations 3:20, which says, "Here I am! I stand at the door and knock. If anyone hears my voice and opens the door, I will come in and eat with him, and he with me." Say something along these lines: "Our front door will always be an open door. Through this door we leave the outside world to enter a place of safety and refuge not only for our children but also for friends, neighbors, and anyone who has a need. For those of us who live inside, it's also a door to the outside world, where we will go and serve Christ at work, at school, and at play. And this door will always be open to Jesus who is the center of our home."

Move inside to the living room or family room. Read John 13:34, 35, which says, "A new command I give you: Love one another. As I have loved you, so you must love one another. By this all men will know that you are my disciples, if you love on another." Then say something like, "This room is where we will spend a lot of time together as a family. Here we will have conversations, watch television, read books, play games, and visit with friends. Our desire is that this room will always be filled with love—love for each other and love for Christ."

Move to the kitchen and dining room. Join hands around the dining room table and read John 6:27, which says, "Do not work for food that spoils, but for food that endures to eternal life, which the Son of Man will give you." Then say, "Here in this kitchen and dining room, we will come each day to prepare our meals and eat them together. Every day we will give thanks to God for his gracious provision of our needs."

Move to one of the bedrooms. Read Psalm 4:8, which says, "I lie down and sleep in peace, for you alone, O Lord, make me dwell in safety." Then say, "Each day concludes in these bedrooms. Our prayer is that every night we can find the peace and quiet, the rest and restoration that our bodies need, after each day of serving the Lord. It is also in these rooms where we will dedicate time each day for personal reflection and quiet times with God."

Move to a guest bedroom. Read Romans 15:7, which says, "Accept one another, then, just as Christ accepted you, in order to bring praise to God." Then say, "We intentionally have a room set aside to welcome and accept anyone who is here for a visit or who needs a place to stay."

Move to the computer room, library, or study. Read Proverbs 4:5, which says, "Get wisdom, get understanding; do not forget my words or swerve from them." Then say, "This is where we will read books, do homework, run our business, pay bills, make important decisions. Our prayer is that everything we say and do in this room will bear fruit and bring glory to God."

You can conclude your service back in the living room with prayer and a time for refreshments. Again, feel free to change this outline to fit your home and family. Add rooms or subtract them. Plan this event well in advance, be creative, have fun with it, and let this be a memorable family affirmation of your faith and commitment to raise godly children.

QUESTIONS FOR REFLECTION AND ACTION

1 | Read Joshua 24:14, 15 again. In this passage, Joshua mentions just a few of the false gods that existed at that time. What are some of the false gods that exist now?

2 | In the Joshua 24 passage, Joshua publicly declares his commitment to serve God. Do you think a public declaration of your family's commitment to serve God is necessary? If so, how could you take that step?

3 | Joshua's commitment to serve the Lord began with himself. What are you personally doing to grow spiritually?

____ I attend worship on a regular basis.

____ I attend Bible studies or classes on a regular basis.

____ I read my Bible daily.

____ I pray daily.

____ I read books that help me grow spiritually.

____ I practice disciplines of the faith such as fasting and solitude.

____ I've asked other Christians to pray for me and hold me accountable.

____ I give generously to God's work.

____ I'm involved in a ministry to others.

____ Other: _____

4 || Joshua also made a commitment on behalf of his whole family—
". . . and my household (NIV)"; "and my family" (*The Message*). This
included his wife and children and perhaps others in his household as
well. Do you think it's possible for us to make a commitment on behalf
of our families today? Explain why you believe what you believe.

5 || Below are some goals many parents have for their children. Which are
most important to you? Give an honest assessment of these parenting goals to this point in your life, ranking them from 1 to 10 (1=least
important, 10=most important). Learn what you can about your priorities from this list.

___ to stay healthy
___ to develop her/his talents
___ to get a good education
___ to have a strong faith in Jesus Christ
___ to perform well in athletics
___ to be popular with his/her friends
___ to be financially secure
___ to develop good moral values
___ to get a good job
___ to find a good husband or wife

6 || Write out a parenting goal for each of your children. Who or what would
you like them to become when they eventually leave home?

THREE

connection

The Internet has changed our lives. With a computer and a high-speed network connection, I can watch videos, listen to music, get directions, find old friends, send text messages, organize my photo collection, sell my old junk, make phone calls, get immediate information, and do research on almost any topic. Much of the communication I do these days is done on the Internet.

That was not true just a few years ago. Remember dial-up modems? (If you still use one, my sympathies go out to you.) It took a lot of patience in those days, waiting for our computers to connect to the Internet while they whistled, beeped, and screeched like someone scratching fingernails on the blackboard or aliens invading from outer space. Once you finally got connected, it would last until someone in the next room picked up a telephone receiver and tried to dial out. It was frustrating and difficult to say the least.

The Internet is a powerful tool and an incredible resource, but you need a high-speed connection to take advantage of it. To take advantage of your role as a parent who wants to pass his or her Christian faith on to your children, you also need a strong connection to your kids. You want a high-speed, broadband, always-on connection that allows you instant and ongoing access to the hearts and minds of your children.

speeding up by slowing down

So how do you establish a meaningful connection with your children? By giving them more of the most valuable possession you have: your time. To children, love is a four-letter word, and it is spelled T-I-M-E. When you give a child your time, you're giving them something that money and things simply cannot buy. You're giving them yourself, which is worth more than anything.

Three children were overheard on a playground. "My daddy is in Washington this week, meeting with a senator," said the first child. "My daddy is in London, making his company millions of dollars," the second child replied. "Well," said the third child in the group, with a big grin on his face, "my daddy is at home."

There's no question that in today's busy world, time is in short supply and, more often that not, children don't get their fair share of it.

You've probably heard the saying "children want our *presence*, not our *presents*." This is so true. Kids aren't that impressed with the stuff we give them or the "quality of life" that we're able to provide for them. What they really want from us is our time. Let's face it, the biggest problem most parents face today is not a financial crisis, a health crisis, or a job crisis, but a time crisis. According to recent studies conducted by the U.S. Department of Labor, the average American parent only spends fifteen minutes a day playing with their children and less than three minutes a day reading or talking to them.[10] A similar study in the United Kingdom recently found that working parents spend only nineteen minutes a day, total, with their children. When you consider that there are twenty-four hours in a day, that amounts to only 1 percent of the day that the average parent is spending with

> **LUNCHBOX DEVOTIONS**
>
> If your kids take lunch to school regularly, occasionally pack a handwritten prayer, Bible verse, or word of encouragement for them to read when they're having lunch. Advice: Keep the note short; lunches aren't that long, and their friends are hanging around too. Don't write a three-page letter, in other words.

their children. Things may not be that bad in your home, but there's no question that in today's busy world, time is in short supply and, more often than not, children don't get their fair share of it.

Let's be real. Busyness is killing the souls of many families. As my colleague and good friend Jim Burns has put it, "If the devil can't make you bad, he'll make you busy."[11] Marriages are disintegrating and children are falling through the cracks simply because we have bought into the notion that doing more and having more is what matters the most. I'm convinced that many young people today gravitate toward at-risk behaviors like sexual promiscuity, drug and alcohol abuse, and other dangerous activities not because they have bad parents but because they have absent parents.

> === FAMILY FUN ===
> ## ❧ A NIGHT AT THE MOVIES ❧
> Choose a movie that you can watch together as a family (at the theatre or at home) and discuss it afterward. What was the main idea or moral of the story? How true was it to real life? Who was the hero? What are some of the positive takeaways from the movie? These all make great discussions with your kids.

High-speed connections are wonderful for getting on the Internet, but high-speed *living* can be devastating to your family as well as to your relationship with God. It's safe to say that the best and perhaps the only way to establish a high-speed connection with your kids is to *slow down* the pace of your life.

I've learned from experience that you can't just have good intentions about leading your family spiritually. Just as you need a commitment, you also need a connection with your kids, and this requires time. Raising children in the faith is about setting and adjusting priorities, deciding what's important, and letting the other stuff go. When we decide that something is important enough to us, we usually find a way to get it done. Every parent can set aside time to spend with their children, but it doesn't happen automatically. If your goal is to raise children who love God with all of their heart, mind, and soul, then you'll need to slow down enough to speed up the connection you have with them.

take time to hang with your children

From time to time, parents will ask me this question: "Is it better to give children *quantity* time or *quality* time?" My answer is usually "yes." I'm not trying to be funny or evasive with that answer. The truth is, both quality and quantity time are extremely important to children. Consider these two scenarios:

Jim Davis believes in quality time. When he gets home from work at 6 in the evening, he gulps down his dinner and then finds his son, Jeremy. "Hey, let's play a little ball!" he announces, and they head for the backyard, where they toss a ball around for a few minutes. While playing catch, Jim asks his son how his day went, and they chat briefly about school and friends. Then Jim shares with Jeremy a Bible verse that came to mind during the day and how he applied it to his life. After a few more tosses of the ball, Jim says, "Well that was great son, but I have a meeting at 7, so let's pick this up again tomorrow, OK?" Dad rushes off to his meeting and Jeremy goes back to his room to do homework and play video games.

Mike Houser believes in quantity time. He wakes up on Saturday morning and announces to his son, Justin, that he's going to spend the day at home so they can be together. They start off by doing a few chores around the house, then they order a pizza and spend the afternoon in the family room eating snacks and watching college football games. They don't say much to each other except to exchange comments about the games. By the time dinner rolls around, they've spent more than seven hours together.

Which example do you think is the better approach? Mike has spent quantity time without a lot of quality, and Jim has managed a few minutes of quality time while leaving his son cheated in the quantity department. If I were forced to choose between these two extremes I would definitely take the second. You can't really get quantity *or* quality time if you're not there. Nor can you plan or predict quality time. The only thing you can plan is quantity time and hope that some quality time emerges.

When my two sons were growing up, I realized that my life was busy (as was theirs) and we needed some time, one-on-one, to just be together and talk. So when my son Nathan was entering the seventh grade, I asked if he would like to go out for breakfast once a week with me. He was very enthusiastic about that (he loves to eat out!) and we chose Wednesday mornings. Every Wednesday of his seventh-grade year, we had breakfast together at Janet's Café, not far from the school he attended. The following year, we did it again. This continued all the way through high school. When he got his driver's license (and a car to drive), we took two cars. For six years straight, we did breakfast together almost every week. When my son Corey reached junior high age, we did the same thing—on Thursday mornings. I made a promise to myself that our conversations would be positive, no nagging about chores or things they've done wrong. Instead, I wanted to find out what was going on in their lives and give them some insight into mine.

I made a promise to myself that our weekly conversations would be positive, no nagging about chores or things they've done wrong. Instead, I wanted to find out what was going on in their lives and give them some insight into mine.

I wish I could tell you that every week we had these incredible conversations during which I was able to communicate insights and wisdom from my years of experience and that I also regularly shared amazing truths from God's Word. On the contrary, we rarely had serious conversations like that. Most of the time, we just had breakfast. But there were a few occasions when I would leave one of those breakfast meetings feeling like something very special had taken place between my son and me. It was a *quality* moment that just wouldn't have happened had there not been a sufficient *quantity* of moments to make it possible. I've learned that you can't plan or program quality time. All you can do is provide the environment and the opportunity for it to happen.

A man took his son fishing one morning. After they got home later in the day, the man's wife asked him, "How was your day of fishing?" The man replied, "Not too good. Our lines constantly got tangled up. I lost several hooks and an expensive lure. The weather was miserably hot. Ants got into our lunch. On top of that, we didn't catch anything. Basically, the day was a total loss."

When the wife asked her son the same question, he replied, "Me and Dad really had a lot of fun, Mom! I think today was one of the best days of my life!"

I've always loved how the apostle Paul compares his ministry to the church at Thessalonica with how a dad connects with his kids.

"We dealt with each of you as a father deals with his own children, encouraging, comforting and urging you to live lives worthy of God, who calls you into his kingdom and glory" (1 Thessalonians 2:11, 12).

The word *comforting* in that passage comes from the Greek verb *parakaleo*, which is frequently translated "to come alongside." It's the same word that's used to describe the Holy Spirit (the "Comforter") who is present with Christians at all times. There is a sense in this verse that Paul understood just how important it is for parents as well as pastors to be present in the lives of those they want to influence—to *be there*. You can't lead someone to love and serve God from a distance.

Jim Burns, in his book *How to Be a Happy, Healthy Family,* writes:

Your children regard your very presence as a sign of caring and connectedness. The power of being there makes a difference in a child's life. This sounds so simple, but don't underestimate the positive message you are giving your kids by watching those games, driving them all around the county, or the hundreds of other ways you are present in their lives. You don't have to be physically present with your kids 24/7, but your presence in their lives gives them a greater sense of security than almost any other quality you can offer them. All studies on positive family living tell us that the results are well worth it when families engage in meaningful times together. Soccer moms, it's worth it. Dads who leave work early to watch the game, it's worth it. Single parents, as tired as you may be, if you continue to find the time to go on special outings with your kids, you will reap the benefits now and later in your family life."[12]

Ask your kids what they would like to do. Let them set the agenda. Usually they'll suggest things that don't cost much money—just time. Take them to the park. Take the little ones to a playground. Take them to the zoo. Play with them in the yard. Go fishing. Do something. Having a family means being together and doing the kinds of things that promote togetherness and connect you to your kids.

I've always loved how the apostle Paul compares his ministry to the church at Thessalonica with how a dad connects with his kids.

One father I know gave his son a coupon book for Christmas containing 365 coupons, each worth one hour of the father's time over the course of the following year. His son could redeem those hours however he wished. It was without question the best present that boy ever received from his father.

take time to encourage your children

I don't know about you, but I love to be around people who like me, who say nice things about me and are generous with words of praise and affirmation. I gravitate toward people like that and hang on their every word.

On the other hand, I hate being around people who are constantly pointing out my faults, criticizing everything I do, and nagging me about everything I do wrong. I avoid these people and pay as little attention to what they have to say as possible.

So it is with our children. If you want a high-speed connection with your kids, take time to encourage them. That will open up the door to effective communication with them.

Take time? Yes, encouragement takes time. If you aren't present in the lives of your children—spending quantity time with them—you probably won't notice when they do something that deserves affirmation and praise. So much of what children do goes largely unnoticed by their parents.

When I conduct parent seminars, I often teach the principle "catch your kids in the act of doing something good." I've also heard it put this way: "Get *off* your kid's back and *on* your kid's team!" It's so easy to only focus on the things that kids do wrong. Something falls to the floor and shatters, a door slams, a bad report card comes home, a mess has to be cleaned up, a hurtful remark is made, someone tattles. Those things are easy to catch. But it takes effort and a lot more time to catch your kids doing something good. The only way you can do that is to spend time with your kids and give them your attention.

If you aren't present in the lives of your children, you probably won't notice when they do something that deserves affirmation and praise. So much of what children do goes largely unnoticed by their parents.

Remember that your presence in your children's lives is in itself a huge encouragement and affirmation to them. There are many children—teenagers especially—who get themselves into trouble simply because they know it's the best way—and sometimes the *only* way—to get their parents' attention. If they can't get the attention of their parents by doing something good, they'll do something bad. You don't want to send the message to your children that they need to misbehave in order to get your attention.

I learned many years ago that encouragement and affirmation don't come naturally for most parents.

A youngster about eight years old received a good grade on a report that he had completed at school and proudly

> ❧ LISTEN AND LEARN ❧
>
> Take time to find out what songs your teens are listening to on the radio, on MTV, or downloading to their MP3 players. Listen to the words of those songs. If you can't understand them, you can probably find the lyrics on the Internet. Ask these questions of your teen and of yourself: What is the song saying? Does it support our values or undermine them? Should I support this artist by listening to this song or buying this music? What should my response be? Rather than telling your teenager what he or she should listen to, it's best if you can teach them how to listen to music and make good choices.

brought it home to show his parents. His mother congratulated him on the accomplishment and gave him a special after-school treat. Knowing that his father would be coming home for dinner, he put the report on the dining room table, right on top of his father's plate. When the dad finally got home from work and took his place at the table, he noticed the boy's report laying across his plate. He tossed it on the floor, growling, "That doesn't belong on my plate!"

This father didn't mean any harm—in fact, he was normally a very gracious and loving dad—but on this particular occasion he crushed the spirit of his young son. In fact, the memory of that day has remained vivid with the boy for more than fifty years. I know—because that boy was me.

I've discovered I'm a lot like my dad. Despite my best efforts, I've failed more than once to notice the positive things that my children did. It's much easier for me to notice when they mess up. That's even more true when you have perfectionist tendencies like mine. For a number of years I worked as a book and magazine editor—one of those people who look for mistakes and then spend all day correcting them. Unfortunately, one of the occupational hazards of being an editor is that you often go home and edit your wife, your kids, your house, and your dog. You keep right on looking for things to correct.

> ### FAMILY TRADITIONS
> ### ❧ SPIRITUAL BIRTHDAYS ❧
> Why not celebrate each person's spiritual birthday on the anniversary of the day they were confirmed or made the decision to make Jesus Lord of their life? If you know these dates, a simple celebration—like lighting a candle on the dinner table or saying a special prayer of blessing—can reaffirm commitments that were made to serve and follow Christ.

I remember the time a friend at church came up to me and mentioned what a wonderful young man my 11-year-old son Nathan was turning out to be. I looked at this person like he had lost his mind, wondering if he had my son mixed up with somebody else's kid. Was this person really referring to the same youngster whose bedroom looked like a garbage dump, who talked back to me when I asked him to do his chores, who got a poor grade because he lost his homework assignment, who was constantly leaving my tools out in the driveway to rust?

Yes, in fact it was the same kid. Someone else noticed Nathan doing something good when I didn't.

Maybe you're a naturally positive and affirming person, but I know I'm not. I've had to work at it and I'm guessing that you probably need to do the same. Here are a few tips that I've found helpful.

Smile when you greet your kids. A smile communicates acceptance, approval, delight, and joy. Are those the things you want your child to associate with you? Then notify your face! There will be times when you want to communicate something different (disapproval of a behavior, for example), but be careful that the first message you send to your children is always one that says "I love you."

Bless your children with words. I've heard parents comment, "I really don't know how to communicate to my child how much I love him."

Actually, the best way is to use words. Just say nice things to your kids once in a while. Say "please" and "thank you" and "I love you" and "I'm proud of you." Don't assume your kids know you love them just because you do a lot of loving things for them. Tell them to their face (along with your actions to back it up) and they'll get the message.

Be specific. Affirmation is always most effective when you look for specific behaviors to praise. For example, it's better to say "Thanks for helping bring in the groceries" than "You've been a good kid today." Being a good kid is certainly positive, but does that mean he's not a good kid if he doesn't help with the groceries?

*Yes, in fact it was the same kid. Someone else noticed
Nathan doing something good when I didn't.*

Look for qualities of character you can praise. If you notice your child being particularly helpful or courteous or courageous or inventive, mention it. Praising character traits—the things that are on the inside—are worth more than flattery (praising only things on the outside *without* taking into account what's on the inside).

Don't worry about the response you get. Sometimes we wish kids would say "thank you," "you're welcome," or "Gosh, Dad, I really appreciate those words of encouragement." Here's an important piece of advice: *Forget about it.* Kids don't know how to respond, but that doesn't mean they don't want—and don't soak in—the affirmation. Keep doing it anyway. With older children and teenagers, I've found that it's best to say something nice to them and then just walk away. A friend of mine calls this dropping love bombs on your kids. Release that word of encouragement and then fly away. Don't put your kids in the awkward position of having to say "thank you" or say something that sounds really lame.

Praise progress, not perfection. Sometimes we withhold praise from our children because they didn't get it exactly right. Kids rarely do. They usually can't do anything as well as their parents, and their parents—being the perfectionists they are—refuse to give them their approval until they do. Look for small steps in the right direction, attempts to do well, even if they don't get it perfect.

Praise publicly. Even though kids will sometimes act shy and pretend they're embarrassed by public praise, deep down they love it when parents brag on them to friends or extended family. When kids know that they have a reputation outside the home to live up to, they just might do it!

A friend of mine calls offering random words of encouragement dropping love bombs on your kids. Release that word of encouragement and then fly away.

Express your encouragement with physical affection. Jim Burns often refers to this as "parenting with AWE." AWE stands for *affection, warmth,* and *encouragement.* Some of us grew up in homes where physical affection (hugging, kissing, touching) was never practiced, and our children and grandchildren today are especially in need of physical touch from their parents. They live in a world that has over-sexualized physical affection and they have few opportunities to experience physical closeness to someone else in a healthy way. I'm convinced that many young people (girls especially) engage in promiscuous sexual behavior to compensate for the lack of physical intimacy they might have received at home in an AWEsome family environment.

In the Bible passage we looked at earlier in this chapter (1 Thessalonians 2:11, 12), Paul describes a good parent as an encouraging parent. Effective communicators and ministers of the gospel know that they can't criticize and scold their audiences and expect a healthy response to their message. In the same way, parents who want to pass their faith on to their children are parents who are generous with loving encouragement.

Many parents take time each day to bless their children by laying hands on the child and saying a prayer or short blessing that encourages them and reminds them of who they are. For some tips on blessing your children, see the sidebar that follows.

❧ BLESSING YOUR CHILDREN ❧

When parents bless their children every day, good things happen. Some parents give their children a formal blessing every day—or just on special occasions—and these become part of their children's identities as they grow into adults. As Scripture says, "The tongue has the power of life and death, and those who love it will eat its fruit" (Proverbs 18:21).

A blessing can be as simple as a prayer for your kids as you send them off to school or tuck them into bed. Or you can compose a special blessing for your individual children, based on your hopes for them, their unique attributes, or the meanings of their names. Here are some examples:

- "Jennifer: You have brought joy into our lives and you bring joy into the lives of others as well. May everyone who knows you see the light of Jesus that shines from within, for you are God's special handiwork. Amen."

- "William: You are a leader for God, the firstborn of many. You are a Determined Protector and a Famous Warrior. God's hand is upon you in a mighty way. Amen."

- "David: You are the beloved of God. On this day and every day, may you share God's love, do his will, and bring glory and honor to his name. Amen."

- Or you can pray the traditional Aaronic Blessing. Here, it's adapted slightly from its original use, found in Numbers 6:22-27:

  May the Lord bless you and keep you.
  May he cause his face to shine upon you.
  May he smile upon you and grant you peace.

Traditional blessings usually involve touch, perhaps placing your hand on the forehead of the child, or on a shoulder, or holding the child in your arms. Jesus himself took children in his arms and blessed them (Mark 10:16).

I know one mother who, every day as her children leave for school, makes the sign of the cross on her children's foreheads with her index finger and says, "May the Lord Jesus be with you today, _____. I love you." Your style may not be quite that formal and may look different. But children *are* impacted. That particular mother's children wouldn't think of leaving home without their mother's blessing.

It always saddens me when I hear young people describe God as angry, spiteful, condemning, distant, or someone who just doesn't like them very much. Where do you think they got this distorted image of God? More often than not, they describe their parents the same way. If we want to lead our children to love and serve God, we need to understand that when they hear our voices, they also often hear the voice of God.

take time to listen to your children

Listening is another way we demonstrate to children something about the attributes of God. I've talked with young people who say they have a hard time praying because they find it hard to believe that the creator of the universe is there to listen to them. Why would God listen to them when their own parents won't? When we listen to our children, we open up to them the possibility that God listens to them also.

Where do you think they got this distorted image of God? More often than not, they describe their parents the same way.

It's been said that listening is the language of love, which might explain why God gave us two ears and one mouth. Listening often communicates more than talking does. When we stop what we are doing and really pay attention to what another person has to say, we're saying more with our ears than we ever could with our mouths.

Some time ago my family lovingly informed me that I am a lousy listener. (At least I *think* that's what I heard them say.) As much as I hate to admit it, I am guilty as charged. I know that I quite often fail to listen to my wife or my kids like I should. Thankfully, I discovered early on that this is not a terminal condition; there is a cure. Listening is a skill that anyone can get better at if they want to—Lord knows, I've tried. There are dozens of books on the market that teach such methods as active listening, reflective listening, and attentive listening, but one of the simplest and most helpful strategies I've learned is called FAD. It's an acronym that stands for *focus, accept,* and *draw out.*

Focus means to stop whatever you are doing and give the person who is speaking your complete attention. Put the paper down, turn off the TV, face the person, make eye contact, and zero in. This is not an easy thing to do, especially with children.

Some of the best teaching on this subject appears in Scott Peck's best-selling book *The Road Less Traveled*:

> The principal form that the work of love takes is attention. . . . And by far, the most common and important way we can exercise our attention is by listening. Listening, no matter how brief, requires tremendous effort. First of all it requires total concentration. You cannot truly listen to anyone and do anything else at the same time. If a parent wants to truly listen to a child, the parent must put aside everything else.

Peck goes on to describe how difficult it can be to listen to a child because the child will usually be talking about things that have no inherent interest for the adult. "Consequently, truly listening to a child of this age is a real labor of love," he writes. "Without love to motivate the parent, it couldn't be done."[13]

Peck goes on to describe how difficult it can be to listen to a child because the child will usually be talking about things that have no inherent interest for the adult.

Accept means to express an attitude of warmth and encouragement while we listen to our children. It means showing a real interest in what they're saying. Sometimes we communicate this with body language, a smile, raised eyebrows, learning forward, expressing appropriate emotions, or by responding to what they have to say with words of surprise or laughter or concern.

FAMILY DINNERS

❧ QUESTION OF THE DAY ❧

Take turns thinking of a "question of the day" to ask everyone at the dinner table. The only rule is this: any question that you ask, you must answer yourself. This is a good one for working on those listening skills!

Draw out means asking questions, probing, and exploring what the child is saying to you. The objective of drawing out is to communicate to the child that you are so interested in what they have to say that you want to hear more. "Tell me more, tell me more!" Like the performer who gets an encore, a child who is encouraged to share more feels affirmed and loved.

Listening is of vital importance to the process of passing faith to your children. The more you listen to your children, the more you'll learn about them. You'll learn what they already know and what they don't know. You'll learn what questions they are asking and what they are interested in. No two children are alike, and the only way you'll know what makes your child different from all other children is to give him or her a generous amount of your attention. More importantly, the more you listen to them, the more they will talk and share their lives with you, and the more willing they'll be to listen to you and give you the same kind of respect that you give them. This is how you create a true high-speed connection to the hearts and minds of your children.

Let me say here that you can listen not only with your ears but also with your eyes. One father told me at a parent seminar that he kept a notebook of observations that he made on each of his four children. He would just watch them—sometimes at a distance—observing them carefully, giving them his attention. Then, at the end of the day, he would write down a few things that caught his eye. His purpose, he told me, was simply to learn to love his children better and to better understand their unique qualities and needs.

take time to talk with your children

For many of us, this is the easy one. We may find it difficult to spend time with our kids, encourage our kids, or listen to our kids, but we don't have a problem telling them what's on our minds. We have warnings, commands, reprimands, and instructions of all kinds that we want to communicate to our kids. We may call it talking but our kids are more likely to call it nagging.

The more you listen to your children, the more you'll learn about them. You'll learn what questions they are asking and what they are interested in. No two children are alike.

That's not what I'm talking about here. But in defense of nagging, let me just say that sometimes nagging can be necessary. My parents were fond of the old saying "halitosis is better than no breath at all" and I think it applies here. Sometimes nagging is better than no talk at all. I've heard parents say "Well, I don't feel comfortable talking with my kids about (sex/drugs/alcohol/friends/school/God) because it all sounds like nagging." Truth is, we need more parents who are willing to nag if that's what it takes to teach our kids right from wrong and how to stay on the right path. Nagging, of course, is not the best way to instruct children, but it's better than keeping our mouths shut.

But you don't have to nag . . . or preach . . . or lecture. You just have to talk, to engage your kids in respectful, frequent conversation similar to the kinds of conversations you have with anyone else. Notice that this is talking *with* your children, not talking *at*, *to*, or *for* them. If you take time to establish a high-speed connection of regular conversation with your kids, you'll be able to instruct your children in the faith and teach them how to love and serve God in a natural and non-nagging sort of way.

You don't always have to say something profound when you talk with your children. Just talk. Keep those communication lines open with lots of conversation that is normal and natural.

One of my favorite writers on child and family issues is Dr. David Elkind. He advises parents to "talk, don't communicate" with their children.

In my opinion, the term communication has been much overused in the literature on parenting. We are told we need to communicate with our offspring, and we are often given various formulas for saying things in the right way.

Elkind points out that as parents we often worry too much about the content of what we're saying to our children and how we say it. This can paralyze us. "Rather than learn to follow a specific script . . . we need simply to *talk*," Elkind writes.[14]

In other words, you don't always have to say something profound when you talk with your children. Just talk. Keep those communication lines open with lots of conversation that is normal and natural. Then when you need to communicate something, you'll have free and open access to the hearts and minds of your children. If you only talk when you want to "communicate" with your kids, they will likely put up a defensive barrier and you will find yourself in the uncomfortable and awkward position of trying to maneuver your way around it.

You may find it hard to believe, but most kids do want to have conversations with their parents. At a recent seminar, I asked parents to suggest some times when they've been able to have good conversations with their kids. One mom shared that she took advantage of the time they spent in the car driving to and from school. And then she offered this suggestion: "Whenever we're in the car together, we have a rule to always turn off our cell phones."

I thanked her for the good idea (it makes a lot of sense) and continued the seminar. After the seminar was over, the youth minister at that church came up to me and said, "Wayne, let me tell you the rest of the story behind that mom's comment about the cell phone rule. Last year, her middle school daughter decided to dress up as a cell phone for our youth group Halloween party. She made the costume herself. She was a walking, talking cell phone. When her mother asked, 'Why on earth do you want to be a cell phone?' her daughter replied, 'Because then maybe you'll talk to me.'"

The more we talk with our kids, the more likely we will have the opportunity to instruct them in the faith. Let's look at 1 Thessalonians 2:11, 12 again. When Paul compares his ministry to how a father deals with his children, he observes that good fathers take time *encouraging* (imparting courage and self-confidence), *comforting* (coming alongside), and then *urging* (instructing) their children to walk with God. I believe that the order is significant here. We can't urge or instruct our children until and unless

❧ TURN OFF THE TV ❧

Let's call out one of the biggest things in western culture that keeps us from spending time talking with our children: television. According to new research, the amount of television viewing by children reached an eight-year high in 2009, with children ages two to five watching the screen for more than 32 hours a week on average and those ages six to eleven watching more than 28 hours. Compare that with one hour a week of religious instruction that children from most Christian homes get each week at church or Sunday school.[15]

Don't fail to set limits on how much TV your children watch. Come up with reasonable rules and enforce them consistently. Do not put TV sets in your children's bedrooms. Make sure that your kids cannot access programming for "mature" audiences. Keep a current list of approved and not-approved TV shows and make sure your children know the reasons why such distinctions are made. If you don't control the TV and teach your children how to watch it, it will control you and your family.

we've established a high-speed connection with our encouragement and our presence.

Our ability to truly communicate has everything to do with the kind of relationship we have with our kids. If it's not healthy and inviting, children will pay little attention to anything we have to say, whether it sounds like nagging or not. You know this is true. Your kids always learn much more from teachers at school—even very strict ones—who have taken the time to build a good relationship with them.

Talk with your kids about anything and everything. The more you talk about the seemingly unimportant things with them, the more opportunities you'll have to talk about God's love for them and how to know Jesus and follow him. We can't leave those discussions to Sunday school teachers and youth evangelists. Don't ever think you are unqualified to give instruction in the faith to your kids. You don't need to be a Bible scholar, a Christian educator, or a spiritual giant to lead your children to Christ and help them grow spiritually. Just take time to talk with them and God will give you the words you want to say.

take time to pray for your children

My friend Scott prays for each of his three children every night just outside their bedroom doors. The children are usually sound asleep by the time Scott makes his rounds to pray. Like me, he's a night person, not a morning person.

Our ability to truly communicate has everything to do with the kind of relationship we have with our kids. If it's not healthy and inviting, children will pay little attention to anything we have to say.

When Scott prays for his children, he normally prays in a quiet whisper, barely audible so he doesn't wake his children. But on one particular night, he softly prayed aloud outside his 13-year-old daughter Amy's bedroom door. When he had finished his prayer with "in Jesus' name, amen," he heard the sound of his daughter's voice from behind the door: "Thank you, Daddy."

Scott shared this incident with me a few years ago and said, "I had no idea she was listening to me pray. But I'm convinced now that my prayers for her over the years were worth all the effort." He's right, of course. The Bible tells us that our prayers are always worth it (James 5:16) and that we should never stop praying for our children and our grandchildren (1 Thessalonians 5:17). We have no control over them and the decisions they make or the values and faith that they will eventually adopt as their own. God is the only one who can control outcomes and so in faith we ask God for the desires of our hearts for our children (Psalm 37:4-6), knowing that God loves them even more than we do.

How many times have you heard from Christian leaders that what inspired them to live for Christ was the indelible image of their parents kneeling together in prayer? That was definitely the case for me. I can say with some degree of certainty that one of the reasons why I chose to remain faithful to Christ as I got older was to become the answer to my parents' prayers.

FAMILY PRAYERS

❧ PRAYER WALKS ❧

A prayer walk is a form of intercessory prayer (praying for others) that involves moving to different locations and praying for the needs that might be suggested there. For example, you can walk around your neighborhood and pray for people who live in the homes up and down the street. If you pass a school, pray for teachers and students who attend there. If you walk by a church, gas station, grocery store, government building, or hospital, you can pray for all kinds of people and circumstances represented by those locations.

Prayer walks can be great for a family prayer time because they give you a chance to get out of the house and also to teach children the biblical principle to "pray continually" (1 Thessalonians 5:17).

You can also do a "prayer drive" in your car if you prefer, stopping at various locations where you can pray together. Then cap it off by stopping on the way home at the ice cream shop.

Pray for your children and pray *with* your children (a few ideas end this chapter). There are times when it's difficult or awkward to tell your kids what's on your heart, but you can always tell God what's on your heart. When your children hear your prayers, they will also get the message. You don't want to ingeniously turn your prayers into speeches directed at your children, but you can talk to God in front of your kids and by doing so reveal to them the deepest desires of your heart. When you pray for them specifically, they will hear your love and concern for them as you talk to God on their behalf.

Here are a dozen ways to pray for your kids, with a few Scripture verses to support each one.

- Pray that they will come to know Christ as Savior early in life (2 Timothy 3:15).

> **FAMILY PRAYERS**
>
> **⅔ PRAY AROUND THE HOUSE ⅔**
>
> Have prayer in each room of the house. Each room can represent a different area of concern: bathroom (health), bedrooms (individual family members), kitchen (thanksgiving for food), garage (travels), guest room (friends, relatives), office (work), family room (family unity). This is similar to the home dedication ceremony discussed in chapter two, but something you can do on a semi-regular basis. Adapt this idea to your home.

> **FAMILY PRAYERS**
>
> **⅔ SIREN PRAYERS ⅔**
>
> When I was a child, whenever my parents would hear the siren of a fire truck or police car or some other emergency vehicle, they would stop and say a quick prayer on behalf of the unknown persons who were in need of help at that time.
>
> To this day, I pray whenever I hear a siren. You can do the same as an example to your kids, and pray with them at those times if possible.

- Pray that they will develop a love for God's Word (Psalm 119:9-12).

- Pray that they will always have the desire to please God and to do his will (Deuteronomy 7:9, 30:16).

- Pray that they will always have a hatred for sin (Psalm 97:10).

- Pray that they will be obedient to their parents as children and respectful to authority as young adults (Exodus 20:12; Luke 2:51; Romans 13:1).

- Pray that they will be protected from the evil one in every area of their lives: spiritual, emotional, moral, social, intellectual, and physical (John 17:15).

- Pray that they will use their gifts and talents to serve God (Romans 12:4-8).

- Pray that they will find good friends and mentors who will be a blessing to them and that they won't fall into relationships that would lead them astray (Proverbs 1:10-15).

- Pray for their safety (Psalm 12:7).

- Pray that they will remain pure in their relationships with the opposite sex (Philippians 2:15; 1 Thessalonians 4:3; 1 Timothy 5:22).

- Pray for the one whom God may be preparing now to become their mate for life (Proverbs 18:22; 2 Corinthians 6:14-17).

- Pray that they will grow up to be a blessing to the world and to be all that God created them to be (Psalm 139:13, 14; Ephesians 2:10).

If you want a high-speed connection with your kids, remember that it is going to take time—time to encourage, time to listen, time to talk, and most importantly, time to pray.

QUESTIONS FOR REFLECTION AND ACTION

1 || In 1 Thessalonians 2:6-13, Paul compares his ministry with parenting. What attributes of parenting can you find in this passage?

Which of these attributes are easiest for you? Which can you work on?

2 || List three things that you enjoy doing with your kids.

3 || What time is the best time for you to be with your kids? Why? How do you use that time wisely? In which of these other areas can you be intentional about spending more time with your children?

Bedtime

Mealtime

Vacation time

Ministry time

Game time

Car time

Sick time

Work time

Hobby time

One-on-one time

4 || Write a short note of encouragement to your child and send it by e-mail, text message, or by sneaking it into his or her sock drawer.

5 || On a scale of 1 to 10, rate yourself as a not-so-good (1) to very good (10) listener.

Not-so-good 1 2 3 4 5 6 7 8 9 10 **Very good**

Now, how do you think your kids would rate you?

Not-so-good 1 2 3 4 5 6 7 8 9 10 **Very good**

6 || Look up the following verses and apply them to your family:

Ephesians 4:32

Romans 12:10

1 Thessalonians 5:17

※ ※ ※ ※

As a sort of halfway mark to this book, I encourage you to take this short spiritual legacy inventory, which I use in many of my workshops. Rate yourself as honestly as you can. Here's the best part: This little tool is only for you. Take a look at the areas in which you score low and consider what could change. It would be even better, of course, to do this with your spouse, or, each of you take the inventory and then share answers.

Read the statements below and rate them from 1 ("weak") to 5 ("strong"). This inventory is not a test, but simply a way for you to identify some areas where you might need to grow.

1 || **EXAMPLE:** My child observes me regularly worshiping and serving God.

      Weak 1   2   3   4   5 Strong

2 || **DEVOTIONS:** I read the Bible, pray with, or have a time of devotions with my child at least once each week.

      Weak 1   2   3   4   5 Strong

3 || **CONVERSATIONS:** I have frequent conversations with my child about the Christian faith and how faith relates to everyday life.

      Weak 1   2   3   4   5 Strong

4 || **FAMILY CULTURE:** Our family culture includes traditions, celebrations, and other habits that identify us as a Christian family.

      Weak 1   2   3   4   5 Strong

5 || **CHURCH:** Our family goes to church together regularly.

      Weak 1   2   3   4   5 Strong

6 || **MINISTRY:** My family is involved in a ministry to others on a regular basis.

      Weak 1   2   3   4   5 Strong

7 || **MENTORS:** My child has healthy personal relationships with caring Christian adults outside the home.

      Weak 1   2   3   4   5 Strong

8 || **MEALTIMES:** Our family eats a meal together, with the TV off, at least once a day.

      Weak 1   2   3   4   5 Strong

9 || **ENCOURAGEMENT:** I give my child encouragement (a blessing) every day.

      Weak 1   2   3   4   5 Strong

10 || **PRAYER:** I pray for my child every day.

      Weak 1   2   3   4   5 Strong

content

Near the entrance to PETCO Park, home of the San Diego Padres, there is an impressive bronze statue of "Mr. Padre," Tony Gwynn, who was recently inducted into the Major League Baseball Hall of Fame. Inscribed on the base of the statue is a quotation from Tony's father, Charles:

If you work hard, good things will happen.

I've heard Tony mention that bit of paternal advice from his father on several occasions. He gives his father all the credit in the world for instilling in him the work ethic that led to his becoming one of the greatest hitters in baseball since Ted Williams.

Have you ever wondered how your kids might quote you someday? What guiding principles do you think they will learn from having grown up in your home? What have they learned from you so far?

That can be a sobering question for all of us parents. Sometimes what children learn from us is not at all what we intended to teach them. "When you die, whoever has the most stuff wins," or maybe "God helps those who help themselves." If we don't tell our kids what we believe, they will, in all likelihood, draw their own conclusions from how we live and from the little clues we leave for them here and there.

Why keep them guessing? If we really want our kids to know what we believe, we'll need to take the time to teach it to them. The Christian faith—more so than any other religion in the world—is one that needs to be clearly taught, to be put into words. Perhaps that's why John introduces Jesus to us in his gospel as "the Word" (John 1:1). Jesus is the Word personified. Christianity is more than just an experience. The gospel is not really about how I feel. It's not about how many good deeds we do or services we attend. It's about a person who came to earth, who lived and died on the cross, and rose again on the third day. The Christian faith is about stories, propositions to be accepted or denied, testimonies, announcements. In fact the faith itself is summed up by the word *gospel*, which means news, *good news* to be exact, about a Savior who did something extraordinary for us. We are commanded to preach this good news to the whole world, beginning, of course, in our own homes.

So we can say with certainty that words are very important to the Christian faith, and that's what this chapter is about. What, specifically, is the *content* of our faith—what do we want our children to learn from us?

Recent studies have found that many young people today—even those who grow up in Christian homes—aren't very clear about the content of their faith. From 2001 to 2005, University of North Carolina (now Notre Dame) sociologist Christian Smith led a team of researchers in a remarkable study of teen spirituality in America. From his extensive interviews, he concluded that:

> Most U.S. teens have a difficult if not impossible time explaining what they believe, what it means, and what the implications of their beliefs are for their lives. Many say they simply have no religious beliefs. Others can articulate little more than what seem to be the most paltry, trivial or tangential beliefs. And others express beliefs that are, from the official perspectives of their own religious traditions at least, positively erroneous. . . . Most teens know details about television characters and pop stars, but [they] are quite vague about Moses and Jesus. Most

youth are well versed about the dangers of drunk driving, AIDS, and drugs, but many haven't a clue about their own [religious] tradition's core ideas.[16]

Smith has described the dominant form of religious belief held by many American young people today as "moralistic, therapeutic deism." The creed of this new religion, Smith found, sounds something like this:

1. A God exists who created and orders the world and watches over human life on earth.

2. God wants people to be good, nice, and fair to each other, as taught in the Bible and by most world religions.

3. The central goal of life is to be happy and to feel good about oneself.

4. God does not need to be particularly involved in one's life except when God is needed to resolve a problem.

5. Good people go to heaven when they die.[17]

Moralistic therapeutic deism is not a religion that includes concepts like the grace of God, repentance from sins, or faith in a Savior who died on the cross for the sins of the world. It's not about worshipping a holy and sovereign God, following Jesus, or becoming part of his church. It's centrally about feeling good, being happy, secure, and at peace. As one Protestant girl from Florida, who described herself as conservative, put it, "God is like someone who is always there for you[.] I don't know, it's like God is God. He's just like somebody that'll always help you go through whatever you're going through. When I became a Christian I was just praying and it always made me feel better."[18]

Smith concluded that most of the teenagers he interviewed had never been asked by an adult what they actually believed. If your child was asked what he or she believed, how do you think they would respond? Let me say here that I don't think any of our children should be expected or required to recite the Nicene Creed on demand, although I know a few teenagers who probably could do it. But Christian teenagers, especially those who come from Christian families, should be able to identify a few of the distinguishing characteristics of their faith that makes it different from all other world religions. Our job as parents is to teach these beliefs to them.

what do you believe?

One of the most memorable exchanges between Jesus and the religious leaders of his day is recorded in Matthew 22:34-40. A Pharisee (a religious leader who was extremely strict in following rites and observances) asked Jesus something of a trick question: "Teacher, which is the greatest commandment in the law?" He was undoubtedly trying to trip Jesus up on this question as all of the Ten Commandments were considered by the Pharisees to be of equal importance. No one would dare elevate one above all the others.

Jesus had an answer that was simple and absolutely correct. It was an answer that any Jewish child certainly would have been able to recite from memory. He quoted Deuteronomy chapter 6 as he answered them: "Love the Lord your God with all your heart and with all your soul and with all your mind." This command, known as the Shema in the Hebrew tradition, was the one that Jewish parents were commissioned by God himself to teach their children at least three times a day—when they woke up in the morning, in the middle of the day, and once more when they went to bed at night. These were the words that were nailed to the doorposts of their houses and worn from their garments. Along with "Hear O Israel, the LORD our God, the LORD is one" (Deuteronomy 6:4), these words summarized their creed, their identity, their mission, and what made their religion different from all other religions. In a world of many gods (polytheism), the Jews defined themselves as worshippers of one God (monotheism). Every Jewish child would have been familiar with this creed and its implications for daily living.

Jesus not only recited the Shema correctly, he amended it by adding another command found in Leviticus 19:18: "Love your neighbor as yourself."

We don't have a complete written record of Jesus' childhood and adolescence, but we can be certain that Joseph and Mary obeyed God by impressing upon Jesus this central teaching of the Jewish faith, just as they were instructed to do in Deuteronomy 6. Jesus was well acquainted with the Shema, not necessarily because he was God incarnate, but because it was faithfully taught to him in his home. We sometimes make the mistake of believing that Jesus didn't need instruction in the faith or parents to train him up in the way he should go because he was God in the flesh. But as

> **FAMILY DEVOTIONS**
>
> **THE TEN COMMANDMENTS AND TV**
>
> OK, this doesn't go against what I said earlier about "turn off the TV"! Occasionally, it's a good thing to watch a decent show together. So pick a show, watch it, and then have everyone make a list of how many times you see commandments or other instructions from the Bible broken. Make another list of how many you see being kept. Make a game out of it; compare your lists later. This exercise will train children—and us too—how to always watch TV and other media with a discerning eye.

Christians we believe that Jesus was not only fully God but that he was, at the same time, fully human, setting aside his deity to identify completely with the human race. We can assume, therefore, that Jesus had to do his homework just like all other boys his age. Likewise, he needed parents to instruct him in the faith, just like all children do. Scripture tells us that even though he was God, he was "obedient to [his parents]" (Luke 2:51) and undoubtedly learned a great deal from them.

And like Joseph and Mary, we must impress upon our own children the good news and disciplines of the Christian faith so that they will embrace it and make it their own. This is not a responsibility that we can give to the church or anyone else. We can't leave it to chance or hope that our kids will seek out the truth on their own. We have a commission from God, a commitment we must make, a connection we must establish, and content that has been revealed to us in God's Word that we must teach. If we don't do it, it's highly unlikely that it will be done by anyone else.

This of course means that we have to be familiar with the content ourselves. At a recent Understanding Your Teenager seminar I encouraged parents—as I always do—to talk with their kids about their faith whenever they have the opportunity. "Your teenager needs to hear from your own mouth what you believe," I told them.

A hand went up. "And what do I say?" a mom asked.

"Excuse me?"

"What do I say?" she repeated. "What should I tell my children that I believe?"

I have to admit her question—which was asked in all seriousness—caught me a little off guard. I had made the incorrect assumption that all of the parents in that room knew what they themselves believed and could talk about it. I had no real answer for her. I could only tell her what I myself believed, which I attempted to do in the short time that I had.

Let me mention again that while Christians around the world agree on many things, there are quite a few issues that create the diversity we see within the body of Christ. We don't all have to worship the same way, think the same way, or practice our faith exactly the same way to be part of Christ's body, the church. Christians come in all shapes and sizes, in other words.

That said, do you know with the strength of conviction what you *do* believe? If you aren't sure, I recommend that you take the time to search the Scriptures, talk to your pastor, read some books by authors you trust and respect, and pray. The Bible teaches that the Holy Spirit of God will lead you into all truth (John 16:13) and because the gospel of Christ is the "power of God unto salvation" (Romans 1:16, *KJV*), it also will change your life. It doesn't matter what church you belong to. You don't have to become an expert on Christianity or a Bible scholar to teach your kids what they need to know. Your experience with Christ will speak volumes.

If you want a good starting point for teaching your children about the Christian faith, you can't go wrong with Deuteronomy 6:4, 5 itself. When God gave his instructions to parents to "impress [these teachings] on your children" (Deuteronomy 6:7), what was supposed to be impressed was (1) there is only one God, and (2) you must love God with all your heart, soul, and mind. These two statements—one of them a creed, the other a command—tells us both what to believe and how to behave. Add Jesus' teaching of "love your neighbor as yourself," and you have a starting place for imparting faith to your kids.

If you want a good starting point for teaching your children about the Christian faith, you can't go wrong with Deuteronomy 6:4, 5 itself.

nail it to the doorposts

Whether it's the Apostles' Creed, a statement of faith of your local church or denomination,[19] or something you write yourself, it's important that you identify what you believe so that you can pass it on to your children with clarity, consistency, and confidence. My suggestion, for the purpose of teaching your children, is to summarize what you believe in just a few simple points. Write them down. Most creeds are meant to be memorized and recited frequently. Don't overcomplicate things. The renowned theologian Karl Barth, who wrote hundreds of books and commentaries on the Bible, was asked in his later years to summarize all that he had learned about the Christian faith. He replied with this classic line: "Jesus loves me, this I know, for the Bible tells me so."[20]

Maybe there are Bible verses that comprise the essential truths you want to teach your children. When I was growing up, our home decor could have been best described as Early King James Version! My parents had all kinds of Bible verses adorning the walls, windows, and bookshelves of our home. Whether we were playing games, watching TV, eating dinner, or even taking a "rest" in the restroom, we couldn't help but find ourselves staring at John 3:16, Matthew 6:33, Romans 8:28, or 2 Corinthians 5:17! Scripture was embroidered on wall hangings, displayed in picture frames, and hung on the refrigerator. What my parents believed may not have been nailed to the doorposts of our house, but by the time I left home, it was certainly nailed into my brain.

Maybe you too have a favorite hymn or worship song that expresses your faith in a meaningful and personal way. I've always been fond of the first verse of "Amazing Grace" and of the chorus to "Victory in Jesus," a hymn my family sang together many times both at church and at home. You can have your favorite words framed and literally nailed up somewhere in your house if you want to do so.

FAMILY DEVOTIONS

❧ ABCD BIBLE STUDY ❧

Choose a passage of Scripture to study with your family and then use these easy-to-remember questions to help everyone get the most out of the study.

A—What is the passage *about*?

B—What is the *best* part of this passage?

C—Anything *confusing* about this passage?

D—What does this passage lead us to *do*?

FAMILY TRADITIONS

❧ LEGACY BIBLE ❧

Buy a Bible for your children when they are young and begin writing things in it that you want them to know. Write about yourself, your family heritage, your favorite Bible verses, and your hopes and dreams for them.

When they're old enough to read it and take care of it, give your children the Bible and they can add their own notes to it.

---

family mission statements

Many parents have found it helpful to compose a family mission statement to serve as a kind of Shema for their family. Most people are familiar with mission statements, which are pretty much mandatory these days for businesses, schools, churches, and other organizations. For a business, a mission statement summarizes the company's fundamental purpose. It answers the question "Why do we exist?" not only for employees, but also for the public.

In the same way, a family mission statement answers the question "What is our family all about?" Such a statement is not only for the benefit of family members, but also for anyone who wants to know what makes their family tick.

What my parents believed may not have been nailed to the doorposts of our house, but by the time I left home, it was certainly nailed into my brain.

There are examples of family mission statements in the Bible, although they weren't identified as such. In the book of Genesis we find Noah's post-flood family mission statement, and it came through God's words to his family: "Be fruitful and increase in number" (9:1). Abraham's: We will "keep the way of the Lord by doing what is just and right" (18:19). Joshua's statement: "We will serve the Lord" (Joshua 24:15). David's, in direction given to his son Solomon while on his deathbed, was: We will "observe what the Lord [our] God requires: Walk in his ways, and keep his decrees and commands, his laws and requirements, as written in the Law of Moses" (1 Kings 2:1-3).

A family mission statement is simply an intentional effort on the part of parents to put into words what they believe and value and how they want to raise their children. Some twenty years ago, after reading one of Stephen Covey's leadership books, I went through the process of writing a personal mission statement, which I still carry in my wallet to this day. Whenever I get discouraged or disoriented about what I'm doing or feel a need to check my spiritual pulse, I revisit that little piece of paper and allow it to remind me of the commitments that I've made to myself, my wife, my children, and my God. My mission statement is a promise that I made to live my life with integrity and purpose. A family mission statement does the same thing. If I were raising my children all over again, I would take the time with my wife to compose a family mission statement to provide all of us with a clearer sense of direction for our family life. Here are just a few of the benefits that I believe such a statement can provide for you and your family.

- A family mission statement can help you identify the *center* of your family life. Stephen Covey calls this establishing a sense of true north, the fundamental guiding principles that will be necessary to keep your family on the right track. The reality of true north, Covey writes, gives context and meaning to where you are, where you want to go, and how you will get there.[21] We can assume that for a Christian family the center, or true north, is likely going to be found in God's Word. My friend Tony Campolo has identified his center by saying that he is a "red letter Christian," meaning that he lives his life by the words of Jesus which, in most Bibles, are printed in red ink.[22]

- A family mission statement can provide you with a sense of *direction and purpose*, freeing you from the tyranny of other people and life's circumstances. If you don't have a clearly defined direction as a family, other people, or the crush of circumstances, will tend to set your direction for you. A family mission statement will help you set priorities for yourself and your family.

- A family mission statement can provide you and your family with the *motivation* to live according to your mission as a family. As the saying goes, "Unless you know where you're going, you probably aren't going to get there." For example, if your family mission statement includes "We will never let the sun go down on our anger," you will be more motivated to forgive and to take care of family squabbles and problems that come up from time to time.

- A family mission statement can help *unify* your family. You'll share a common vision. If each of the family members participate in the creation of the statement, the process of making it will draw your family together.

- A family mission statement can serve the function of a family *constitution*. While the Bible serves as the ultimate authority for our creed and conduct, a mission statement can put into words some of those unspoken standards and principles that may need to be clearly affirmed by your family. For example, if your family mission statement includes a line that says "We will never use foul or abusive language in our home," there will never be any doubt regarding where you stand on that issue.

Writing a family mission statement can be a great exercise for you and your family. I've led weekend family retreats where moms and dads together with their children have written family mission statements that they've taken home to frame and hang on their walls. They refer to them frequently or memorize and recite them at mealtimes. Some families print their mission statements on small cards and laminate them so that they can be carried in their wallets. Some have put their mission statements on their computers as a screen saver or posted them on their family's Web site or Facebook page, perhaps the modern-day equivalent to nailing their beliefs to the doorposts of their house.

If I were raising my children all over again, I would take the time with my wife to compose a family mission statement to provide all of us with a clearer sense of direction for our family life.

Mission statements don't have to be long. You may want to create a short version that you can memorize and recite frequently and then a longer version to post in your home, one with more detail and commentary. For example, if your family mission statement is "We are red letter Christians," you'll probably need another document to unpack the meaning of that phrase and provide some application principles. Those could be things like "We will always treat others with kindness and respect, especially those who are considered 'the least of these.'"

Here are a few sample family mission statements, some of which may provide ideas for you.

The Harrison family

"LOVE GOD, LOVE PEOPLE"

"For it is by grace you have been saved, through faith—and this not from yourselves, it is the gift of God" (Ephesians 2:8).

The Robinson family

"'[We are] dead to sin but alive to God in Christ Jesus' (Romans 6:11). This means that our salvation comes by faith in Jesus, who died for our sins on the cross and gives us eternal life.

"'He has risen!' (Mark 16:6). This means that we are a resurrection family. Because he lives, we also will live with joy and thanksgiving in our hearts.

- We love God: This means that we will worship God together as a family and always give him first place in our lives.

- We love others: This means we will live our lives unselfishly, giving of ourselves in service and ministry to others.

- We love ourselves: This means that in humility we will take good care of ourselves and seek to become all that God has created us to be.

- We love God's creation: This means that we will be good stewards of the earth and all the material possessions that God has blessed us with.

- We love the truth: This means that we will always tell the truth and live our lives with integrity and according to God's truth, the Holy Bible."

Here is a simple line drawing that could go with such a family mission statement, which might give you ideas for a drawing to go with your family's statement:

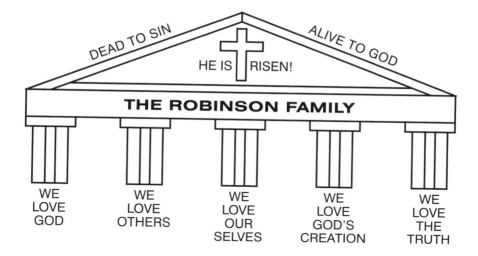

The Murdoch family creed

"We will live each day to the glory of God, with gratitude, discipline, purpose, and joy.

"We will strive to treat each other with love, respect, and humility.

"We will seek God's will at all times."

The Torres family

"Our mission is to love God, to be obedient to him, and to make a positive difference in the world. We will love God by loving each other and honoring each other in word and deed. We will encourage each other to be all that God has created us to be. We will stick together through good times and bad and always be thankful for what God has given us, especially his gift of salvation through Jesus Christ our Lord.

FAMILY DEVOTIONS
FAMILY DINNERS

❧ FAMILY PLACE MATS ❧

As a project make a family place mat for your dinnertimes with your family's "coat of arms." If you don't have a family coat of arms, make one! Use interesting photos, Bible verses, autographs, and the like. Make the original on an 11 x 17 sheet of paper, then have it duplicated and laminated. If everyone makes their own, you can laminate it yourself with supplies from any office supply store.

You can be creative with other ideas, like making place mats for each month with a "verse of the month" on them to read together before each meal.

"Each member of our family is an important part of it and will contribute to the family unselfishly. We will put God first, not money or possessions or prestige. We will worship God as a family every Sunday morning in church. We will pray daily around the dining room table and at other times when we want to seek God's direction and help."

The Dan and Janine Jenkins family

"We believe in God the Father, who by his grace sent his only Son, Jesus Christ, to die on the cross for our sins. By the power of the Holy Spirit, we commit ourselves to love God every day with our hearts, minds, and soul and to love others as we love ourselves."

These sample mission statements are quite different from each other because every family is unique. While Scripture tells us that there is only one Lord, one faith, and one baptism (Ephesians 4:5), we acknowledge that every family is comprised of different people with different talents, interests, personalities, and so on. How we express our faith and talk about it will vary greatly from family to family. Your mission statement should be a reflection of the uniqueness that God has given to you and how you want to train up your children. For example, if your family loves to laugh, you might consider including something humorous. If your family is musical, your mission statement could take the form of a song. The sample mission statements above are only examples of what some people have already done.

FAMILY VACATIONS

❦ TAKE A LEGACY VACATION ❦

For many people a pilgrimage can be extremely strengthening to their faith. That's no doubt why some other world religions require one. Essentially, a pilgrimage is a journey to a place or places that have great spiritual significance to you. It could be visiting where you were born or baptized, a summer camp where you made serious decisions about your spiritual life, a church you attended as a child or teenager, or a place where you served on a mission trip. It could be a journey to the homes or birthplaces of some of your spiritual mentors, or even a trip to the Holy Land. Some families trace their spiritual roots to particular places they can visit and there affirm their faith in a special way. This can be a powerful experience for children to see with their own eyes the places where significant spiritual events took place.

Keep in mind that a mission statement by definition is an *abbreviated* representation of what you believe and value. Your statement shouldn't be long or complicated. While a very short mission statement like "LOVE GOD, LOVE PEOPLE" is probably not going to be sufficient in itself to teach children all they need to know about the Christian faith,[23] it can still point your family toward that goal of

> **FAMILY VACATIONS**
> ### ❧ FAMILY CAMP ❧
> Many Christian conference centers offer family camps where you can spend a week together as a family in a beautiful location and also have times for spiritual refreshment and renewal. Even if you're not a "camping person," do this at least once with your kids. Heck, do it more than once. You won't regret it.

true north. As you recite together and talk about your mission statement, you can help your children learn more about it and how it applies to daily living.

How we express our faith and talk about it will vary greatly from family to family. Your mission statement should be a reflection of the uniqueness that God has given to you and how you want to train up your children.

Remember to make your statement as timeless and "always true" as possible. If you include a statement like "We will never watch TV on Sundays," consider that there is a likelihood you may one day change your mind on that issue or find it hard to enforce, either of which may undermine the integrity of every other part of your statement. It's best to base your statement on universal truths from the Word of God that will never change.

Mission statements can be amended, however. This is an especially good idea when you have young children in the home. Rather than beginning with a long and detailed statement, you might want to start with one that is very simple, like "We love God." Then, in successive years, as the children grow older, you can add new lines. For example:

1. We love God.

2. We love others.

3. We love God's Word, the Bible.

4. We believe Jesus died on the cross for our sins.

5. We will always be thankful for what God has given to us.

6. We will share what we have with others, especially those who are less fortunate.

7. We will be faithful members of Christ's body, the church.

8. We will use our talents and gifts to bring glory to God.

9. We will share Christ with others at every opportunity.

10. We will all live together in Heaven someday.

Remember that family mission statements can take many forms, just like families themselves. There's no one way to compose such a statement, nor are they mandated by God. But the important truth here is that we must be intentional about teaching our children what we believe and find effective ways to repeat and reinforce that teaching throughout their childhood and adolescence until the day they leave home.

❧ FAITH STORIES ❧

Keep your young teens and high school teens every bit as involved in building your family's faith and legacy. If your middle to older children like to be creative with the technology that's available these days, commission them to make a movie about your family's spiritual legacy. Have them interview members of your family, your extended family (grandparents and others), pastors and former pastors, and others who have been spiritual influences on your family.

a word about smaller children

I'm cautious about child evangelism. But I'm also convinced that many children do some of the most intentional seeking of their entire lives while they are still quite young. Children can amaze us with their seeking hearts, even while young; we should always invite their questions and thoughts, even about accepting Christ as Lord, and answer them with wisdom and discernment.

If your children go to Sunday school or Vacation Bible School or some other church-related children's programming, they may be asked to go deeper with their faith, or they may come home asking you new questions. There is no greater privilege for Christian parents than to lead your own children to Christ. Be intentional about this, and always be open to what God may be doing in their hearts. Take every opportunity to present the wonderful message of God's love to your children while their hearts are eager and open.

Remember that family mission statements can
take many forms, just like families themselves.

Your children will have plenty of questions about various terms, so take the time to explain them. They may not understand words like *sin* or *Savior* or *Heaven* or *eternal life*. Don't push children to admit to sin when they don't understand what it means and don't scare them with talk about dying and going to Hell. They probably won't understand why it was necessary for Jesus to die so that they can go to Heaven. Just reassure them that Jesus is alive now and that he wants to be their Savior at the point that they are ready. Remember that you as a parent can introduce your children to many of these biblical concepts in a healthy and nurturing environment over time. Your children will respond in the right way when they are ready and when the Holy Spirit leads them to do so.

1 | Spend a minute or two thinking back to your childhood. What were the core values and beliefs that were taught to you by your parents?

How did they teach them?

2 | How do you think your children will answer the questions below after they've left home?

- My mom/dad's favorite entertainer was _____

  _____.

- My mom/dad's favorite Bible verse was _____

  _____.

- My mom/dad's favorite meal was _____.

- My mom/dad's favorite Bible story was _____.

- My mom/dad's favorite TV show was _____.

- My mom/dad's favorite promise from the Bible was _____

  _____.

3 || Which of the following topics do you believe your children should learn before they leave home? (Choose the top five.)

The attributes of God
The life of Jesus Christ
The Sermon on the Mount
How to get to Heaven
The role of the Holy Spirit
How to be baptized
How to flee from sin and Satan
Heroes of the faith
How to study the Bible
The role of the church
The Ten Commandments
Christian love (1 Corinthians 13)
Christian stewardship (money)
The second coming of Christ
The Communion
The fruit of the Spirit
The Great Commission
The Lord's Prayer
Creation vs. evolution
What the Bible says about sex
The Apostles' Creed
Church history
Discovering your spiritual gifts
Other: _____
Other: _____

4 || If one of your children were to ask, "What does our family believe?", how would you answer—in twenty-five words or less?

5 || To begin the process of writing a family mission statement, make a list of the values, beliefs, and behaviors that you would want to include in it.

6 || If you are a Christian, at what age did you make that decision? _____ Who led you to Christ? _____

communication

Then Jesus took his disciples up to the mountain and he began to teach them, saying, "Blessed are the poor in spirit, for theirs is the kingdom of God. Blessed are the meek. Blessed are those who mourn, for they shall be comforted. Blessed are those who thirst for justice. Blessed are the merciful. Blessed are the pure. Blessed are the peacemakers. Blessed are those who are persecuted for my name's sake. Blessed are those who suffer. Be glad and rejoice, for great is your reward in Heaven."

Then Simon Peter said, "Do we have to remember this?"

And Andrew said, "Should we write this down? I don't have a pencil."

And James said, "Will there be a test on this?"

And Philip said, "When is lunch?"

And Bartholomew said, "Haven't I heard this somewhere before?"

And John said, "The other disciples didn't have to learn this."

And Matthew said, "Can I go to the bathroom?"

And Judas said nothing because he was sound asleep.

Then one of the Pharisees who was standing nearby asked to see Jesus' lesson plan and inquired of him, "Where is thy three-point outline, thy experiential learning strategy, and thy PowerPoint presentation?"

And Jesus wept.

I've always loved this apocryphal version of Matthew 5 because it reminds me so much of all the times I've tried to teach youth, including my own children, incredible truths from the Word of God, only to get bored eye rolls and innumerable complaints. Every teacher knows that even with the best content in the world, unless it is communicated effectively, it's likely to fall flat.

communication principles you can apply at home

How can we best communicate the content of the Christian faith to our kids? Some parents are reluctant to try because they just don't feel qualified. They aren't sure they have the necessary training to be a teacher or know enough about educational theory or developmental psychology to teach their kids about how to love and serve God. They would rather just outsource this job to "professionals who know what they're doing."

But no parent is unqualified to pass faith on to their kids. In fact, if you're a parent, no one is better qualified to teach and nurture your children in the faith than you are. Sunday school teachers, Christian educators, youth pastors, children's workers, and other significant influencers of your kids can support and reinforce what you teach your children, but they will never be able to train up your children in the same way that you can simply by virtue of the fact that *you* are their parent.

Of course, that doesn't mean you can't improve as the primary spiritual trainer of your children. As parents, we should learn all we can about effective teaching so that we can leverage the immense amount of influence that we have with our kids. I've always been impressed with how homeschooling organizations provide so much training and resources for parents who homeschool their children. While the majority of these parents are not professional teachers, they do it with confidence and great effectiveness simply because they take advantage of the resources that are available to them.

As parents, we should learn all we can about effective teaching so that we can leverage the immense amount of influence that we have with our kids.

But you don't have to be a homeschool parent in order to learn the basics of how to communicate effectively with children. Here are a few key principles to keep in mind when you are teaching your children spiritual truth.

principle #1: no child is too young

Remember that it's never too early to start teaching your children about God. Granted, children's understanding of God and spiritual things will change dramatically as they get older, but you'd be amazed by how much a child picks up even before he or she is able to talk. From his high chair, our two-year-old grandson, Jack, absolutely insists that we begin each meal with a prayer. He stretches out his hands and demands "Pray! Pray!" At the end of the prayer, he grins and shouts "A—men!" I wonder how much he understands? As I wrote in the last chapter, it doesn't really matter. What matters is that the indelible tracks of thanksgiving are being planted in his heart, and I'm confident these will shape his life for many years to come.

> ❧ **LETTERS TO YOUR CHILDREN** ❧
>
> If you have young children, make a habit of writing annual—or if you want, monthly—personal letters to them that you can keep in a safe place until they are old enough to read and understand them. Letters can include descriptions of them and the things they did, things you did together as a family, and the dreams you have for them. These letters can be a treasure to your children as they get older. They will also prove an excellent way for your kids to see themselves the way you see them and, hopefully, as God sees them.

principle #2: the more you teach, the more they will learn

Just as there's no such thing as quality time without quantity time, so there's no such thing as quality teaching without quantity teaching. I can't remember a single sermon or Sunday school lesson that I heard as a child, but I know I heard hundreds, maybe thousands of them. The cumulative effect is that I picked up a lot of knowledge about the Bible and about how—and how not—to live the Christian life.

Deuteronomy chapter 6 instructs parents to teach children about God "when you sit at home and when you walk along the road, when you lie down and when you get up," which for the Jews meant three times a day or more. More likely it meant "all the time!" Teaching children about God shouldn't be reserved for one particular time and place each week but for whenever you have the opportunity.

principle #3: every learner learns best in his or her own way

This is one of those self-validating principles that every parent learns shortly after their second child is born. No two children are the same, nor do they respond in the same way. Every child brings to the table his or her own individual personalities, propensities, and preferences when it comes to how they learn best. This can present real challenges for parents who want to effectively pass their faith on to their kids.

Most teachers today have become acquainted with what are generally called learning styles. These are a way of describing how individual students learn best. Just as everyone has a different signature, so everyone has a different learning style—a way of understanding and processing information that is uniquely theirs.

Marlene LeFever, in her book *Learning Styles: Reaching Everyone God Gave You,* identifies four distinct learning styles.[24] Which ones do you think your children might have a preference for?

- *Imaginative learners* learn best by interacting with others. They like to ask a lot of questions, share experiences with others, collaborate, and arrive at a group consensus. They are social and learn best in groups.

- *Analytic learners* learn best by watching and listening, taking notes, and processing information as it is given to them by the teacher. They are deep thinkers, able to solve problems and arrive at conclusions.

- *Common sense learners* learn best when they see the connection between what they are learning and life as they are experiencing it. A key question for them is "What does this have to do with me?" They aren't comfortable learning unless they can apply it and put it into practice.

- *Dynamic learners* learn best when they are being creative. Like common sense learners, they enjoy application, but they also like exploration and adventure. A key question for them is "What can this become?" They aren't as interested in the solution as they are being part of the solution.

Children usually have a preference toward one learning style or another, just as we parents and teachers do. Most people are able to learn in all four styles but find it easier to learn in their own style, which is often a hybrid. What LeFever points out in her book is that most teachers teach in the style in which they are most comfortable, not realizing they aren't communicating very well with their students, who have other needs.

It's not important to remember all of these learning styles or even to identify the preferred learning style of your individual children right away. What's important is that you use enough variety in your teaching that each of your children has opportunities to learn in the way that suits them best.

principle #4: you can't teach a teenager like a toddler

Learning styles not only vary from child to child depending on their individual preferences, they change depending on the child's age.

For example, it's safe to say that most children (up to about age 10) make the best listeners. They learn most effectively with their ears. They love to hear stories and will absorb all kinds of information. It's truly amazing what children learn just by hearing us talk!

Middle schoolers (ten to fourteen) learn best with their eyes. They are primarily visual learners who learn by observation. Through the years, as a middle school youth worker, I've loved exposing young adolescents to what God is doing in the world. Their eyes are being opened and they need to see role models, examples, and illustrations of God's love and transforming power. Much of the teaching we do with middle schoolers seems to go in one ear and out the other, but they don't miss much with their eyes.

On the other hand, high school students learn best by doing. They learn with their hands and feet. They need to be involved or they will become bored, and quickly. That's why effective high school youth ministry gets students involved in leadership, missions, ministry, and service so that they can learn from experience what it means to be a follower of Jesus.

> **FAMILY TRADITIONS**
>
> **❧ KEEP A FAMILY SCRAPBOOK ❧**
>
> Document your family's spiritual journey by taking pictures of meaningful moments like baby dedications, weddings, church activities, holidays, vacations, and more that have great meaning for your family. There are a number of photo-sharing Web sites that will give you the tools for creating very nice scrapbooks with graphics and text to tell the story of your family and your faith in pictures.

Again, the point here is not to categorize children according to age or learning style, but to recognize that we may need a variety of approaches with our kids so that they'll remain motivated and completely engaged in the learning process.

principle #5: don't forget the words

I've always loved the quote that is attributed to Saint Francis of Assisi: "Preach the gospel at all times; when necessary, use words." It's a good reminder to all of us that our actions often speak louder than our words.

But our actions are not the gospel. Only the action that God took by sending his Son to die on the cross for our sins is the gospel. I sometimes hear parents say, "I teach primarily by example. I don't think it's important to talk to my children about God. I just live my faith in front of them and let them figure it out on their own."

Modeling is crucial, of course, but without words your children won't figure out much of anything. As we discussed in chapter four, our faith has *content* and it can only be communicated in words. I don't want my children to just believe in me; I want them to believe in the God of the Bible who has revealed himself not only in nature and the kindnesses of people but also in words. I want my children

❧ CREATE A FAMILY TIME CAPSULE ❧

For a fun family activity, create a time capsule containing various artifacts of your family and faith that you can stash away in a safe place and retrieve at some date in the future. The actual "capsule" doesn't have to be expensive or fancy. A coffee can or a large plastic bottle or other container will work just fine. Decorate it and mark on the outside: "DO NOT OPEN UNTIL (some date in the future)." For fun, you can include the usual kinds of time capsule items: photos, artifacts of pop culture, magazine or newspaper articles, and more. Then have each member of the family write down their favorite Bible verse, a recent answer to prayer, a meaningful experience they've had with God, the name of a spiritual mentor or hero, a prayer they have for the future, and so on. These can be put into envelopes and sealed before inserting them into the time capsule.

Don't bury the capsule in the backyard—it will probably deteriorate, or you might move. Instead, put it in a safe place where you keep other family heirlooms and agree to open the capsule in five, ten, or twenty years. The act of preserving a piece of your family's spiritual journey in this symbolic way can help children to think more long-term about their faith and family heritage.

to be able to articulate what they believe in their own language, which happens to be English. Ultimately, the good news of the gospel of Christ involves words, or more specifically the Word. While it's true that "more is going to be caught than taught," that doesn't mean we shouldn't do all we can to make sure our children know the Bible and know the stories and tenets of the historic Christian faith.

Talk in the normal course of spending time with your kids.
Let them hear what you think—they pay a lot more
attention to what's on your mind than you think.

Scripture commands parents to "Tell it to your children, and let your children tell it to their children, and their children to the next generation" (Joel 1:3).

What if your kids aren't listening? Well, Scripture has a few things to say to them too. A few admonitions from the book of Proverbs:

"Listen, my son" (1:8).

"My son, do not forget my teaching" (3:1).

"Listen, my sons, to a father's instruction" (4:1).

"Listen, my son, accept what I say" (4:10).

"My son, pay attention to what I say; listen closely to my words" (4:20).

"My son, pay attention to my wisdom" (5:1).

"Now then, my sons, listen to me" (5:7).

"My son, keep your father's commands and do not forsake your mother's teaching" (6:20).

"My son, keep my words and store up my commands within you" (7:1).

"Now then, my sons, listen to me" (7:24, 8:32).

True, children aren't always going to be receptive to what we say, but we must keep on saying it anyway. Both sons and daughters need to hear us talk about God. Tell them the stories and the good news that comes from God's Word. As Paul wrote, "Can they believe in the one of whom they have not heard? And how can they hear without someone preaching to them? . . . 'How beautiful are the feet of those who bring good news!' . . . Faith comes from hearing the message, and the message is heard through the word of Christ" (Romans 10:14, 15, 17).

Don't assume they know what they need to know and don't hand this important job over to the church and its various ministry programs. Just because your kids are going to Sunday school or youth group doesn't mean they are learning the foundational stories and lessons they need from God's Word.

You don't have to bore your children with lectures and daily Bible lessons. In fact, please don't! Just take advantage of teachable moments. Talk in the normal course of spending time with your kids. Let them hear what you think—they pay a lot more attention to what's on your mind than you think.

principle #6: reinforce words with concrete

Jesus did a lot of teaching, most of which included the telling of stories (parables) that were concrete illustrations of the truths he wanted his hearers to understand. As I mentioned earlier, middle schoolers especially need those kinds of examples and illustrations to reinforce their learning.

I can still remember the day my father took me to the local mortuary to view the body of a coworker of his who had been electrocuted. Apparently this man didn't take the necessary precautions electricians normally take when working with electrical wires; he was killed instantly under a house. My father, who was a building contractor, had told me many times to be careful when working with electricity, but the sight of this man in a coffin made an impression on me that remains to this day. I am not afraid to work with electricity, but I am one very careful electrician when I do.

You don't have to take your children to a mortuary to make a lasting impression on them. Anytime you can move from the abstract to the concrete by providing examples, demonstrations, and illustrations to drive home the lessons you are teaching, you'll be helping them learn in ways that words can't do alone. Jesus often used such ordinary things as the "lilies of the field" to illustrate his points; these were so memorable that the apostles recorded them in their gospel accounts. We can use all kinds of concrete examples to teach: TV shows, newspaper articles, movies, household items. I've used a glove to teach the idea that "just as a glove comes to life when my hand goes into it, so we come to life when Christ is in us. We can do all things through Christ who gives us strength, just like a glove can do anything that my hand can do."

Of course, the best concrete example you can give your kids is the demonstration of your own life. I know that most of what I learned about living the Christian life from my parents came from observing them day after day. I saw with my own eyes how much my father and mother loved God.

My parents had a very high view of the Bible, and they taught it to us. But I came to appreciate the true value of the Bible by watching my parents read it every day. My parents believed in prayer, and I learned this because I often observed them in prayer. My parents taught me such values as purity, hard work, honesty, service to others, generosity, and gratitude not by giving lectures on these subjects but by putting those values into practice in our home, around the dinner table, in their work, and in how they treated other people. As Tony Evans writes, "It bears repeating again: our kids learn from us mostly by our actions. If our words are different from our actions, our children will give the most weight to what we do."[25] Words are important, but they need to be reinforced with concrete.

principle #7: practice makes perfect

If we want our children to become firm in their faith, they'll need to put it into practice. Regardless of age or learning style, the best kind of learning always comes from direct experience. If you really want to learn something— and remember it—a certain amount of experience has to be involved. Consider the difference between looking at a photograph of the Eiffel Tower in a book and the experience of standing next to the Eiffel Tower in downtown Paris. Or taking the elevator ride to the top! It's an unforgettable experience. You may be primarily a visual or auditory learner, but all learning is enhanced when experience is involved.

More than half a century ago, Edgar Dale, a professor at Ohio State University, did studies to determine how various learning strategies impact retention. The result of his studies was the development of his famous "cone of learning," which is pictured here. What he discovered is that retention increases as the learner moves from reading and hearing (verbal symbols) to actual experience and involvement (doing the real thing).

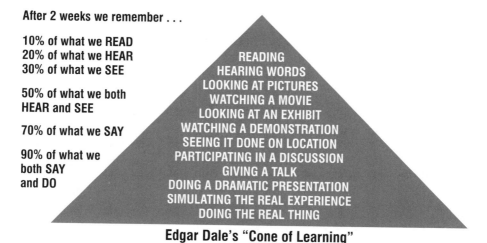

After 2 weeks we remember . . .

10% of what we READ
20% of what we HEAR
30% of what we SEE

50% of what we both HEAR and SEE

70% of what we SAY

90% of what we both SAY and DO

READING
HEARING WORDS
LOOKING AT PICTURES
WATCHING A MOVIE
LOOKING AT AN EXHIBIT
WATCHING A DEMONSTRATION
SEEING IT DONE ON LOCATION
PARTICIPATING IN A DISCUSSION
GIVING A TALK
DOING A DRAMATIC PRESENTATION
SIMULATING THE REAL EXPERIENCE
DOING THE REAL THING

Edgar Dale's "Cone of Learning"

The top of the cone—where you find verbal activities like reading and listening to someone talk—represents the least effective teaching methods. Only 10 to 20 percent of what a person reads or hears is retained. At the bottom of the cone, however, you find what Dale called "direct purposeful experiences," 90 percent of which is retained.[26] This proves the truth of the old saying "Tell me, I'll forget; show me, I'll remember; walk with me, I'll understand."

There is a famous parable told by the Danish philosopher Soren Kierkegaard about a community of ducks who waddled off to duck church one day to hear their duck preacher. The duck preacher quacked eloquently about how God had given every duck wings with which they could fly. With those wings there was nowhere the ducks could not go; there was no God-given task the ducks could not accomplish. With those wings they could soar into the presence of God. Shouts of "Amen!" were quacked throughout the duck congregation. At the end of the service, the ducks quacked to each other about what a powerful, awe-inspiring message they had just heard. And then they all waddled back home.

Doesn't this sound a little bit like the kind of learning that goes on in some of our churches? We hear a lot of exhortation but don't see much change in behavior. Jesus taught that we should be doers of the word, not just hearers. Certainly one reason why is because unless we are putting our learning into practice, we aren't going to remember a thing. If you want your kids to do more than waddle, you'll need to get them up in the air and let them flap their wings a bit. Help them put their faith into practice.

FAMILY SERVICE PROJECTS
❧ TITHE YOUR SATURDAYS ❧

Most families try to do something together on Saturdays when the workweek is over and the kids are home from school. Why not consider tithing your Saturdays by doing a family service project together? That would mean that you would do a family service project once every ten weeks or so—about four or five per year. You can always give above and beyond a tithe, of course, but this might be a good way to get into the habit of serving together as family. Be sure to plan ahead and put the dates on your family calendar. The projects you choose don't have to take up the whole day. You can do something as simple as mowing the lawn or planting flowers for an elderly person or participating in a roadside cleanup project. What you do isn't as important as the experience you have together as a family.

principle #8: happy learners are better learners

It almost goes without saying that when children are learning in an environment where they are comfortable, engaged, and having a good time, they will learn better. Those of us who've been involved in youth ministry through the years know just how true this is. We go out of our way to create engaging and fun activities for young people for the purpose of encouraging learning and spiritual growth.

Years ago a Jewish rabbi told me about an ancient Hebrew tradition that expresses this idea. It's called putting honey on the Torah. To draw children to God's Word, rabbis would put a dab of honey on the cover of the holy book and encourage the children to lick it off, thereby associating sweetness with the Word of God. Whether this is practiced widely today or not I can't really say, but I like the concept. Whenever we incorporate sweetness, affirmation, grace, and good humor into our teaching, our children will likely be much more responsive to it. It's a sad fact that many young people reject their faith later on in life because they associate it more with negative experiences than positive ones. The more we can connect the instruction of our children in the faith with joy and laughter, the more likely our children will be drawn to it for years to come.

FAMILY PRAYERS
⚘ PRAYER DICE ⚘

Here's a way to get your kids more involved in family prayer times. Make a cube that can be rolled like a die; make it out of wood, cardboard, plastic, or Styrofoam and make it any size you want. On each of the six sides, draw a picture that represents the kind of prayer that the person who rolls the die will say. Prayers can be short, with each person rolling the die around the prayer circle. Repeat as many times as you want. Here are some suggestions for drawings you can put on the six sides of the cube, but use your ideas.

- A gift (pray to thank God for the gifts he has given)
- A road sign or map (pray for God's guidance)
- A sad face (pray for someone who is hurting)
- A happy face (pray for something good that happened that day)
- A cross (thank God for our faith and what Jesus did on the cross)
- A flag (pray for your country and its leaders)

You can make a pair of prayer dice by making a second cube with names of family members written on the six sides. Pray for the person whose name comes up with each roll.

You may have noticed that some of the practical ideas in this book, at first, seem silly. Or, that they obviously involve children in fun activities that include candy and ice cream. These are simply examples of putting honey on the Torah. There's nothing at all wrong with occasionally allowing your children to make a connection between a chocolate chip cookie and the sweetness of God's love. Obviously, there comes a time when rewards, entertainment, and other enticements become counterproductive and unnecessary. But children generally do learn best when they are enjoying the learning experience.

> **FAMILY DINNERS**
>
> ❧ **THE BEST PART OF THE DAY** ❧
>
> At dinner every night, play "best part of the day." Someone says "Best part of the day!" and every hand goes up. The last hand that goes up is the person who has to share their favorite part of that day. He or she can then name who goes next until everyone has shared the highlight of their day. At the conclusion, pray and thank God for all the "best parts" that every person mentioned.

> **FAMILY TRADITIONS**
>
> ❧ **MUST-SEE MOVIE NIGHT** ❧
>
> Does your family have a favorite movie that everyone loves to watch together? Pick one night each year when you put it on the big screen (rent a projector and screen if necessary) and watch it together. One example would be to watch the classic *It's a Wonderful Life* on December 1 every year to help everyone get into the Christmas spirit!

family culture

A good deal of research has been done on the faith development of children, and there is wide consensus that most children (and youth) begin their faith journeys by simply adopting the family culture that they grew up with. By *family culture* I'm referring to the normal routines of family life, the daily habits, priorities, and practices that you may not even realize you have. Every family has its own way of doing things that defines its family culture. You can tell a lot about a family by observing that culture.

When I was growing up, my family was very different from other families—but I didn't know that. I thought my family was pretty normal. I thought everybody took a bath on Saturday night (in preparation for church on Sunday morning). I thought everybody said prayers at the dinner table. I thought everybody went to Wednesday night prayer meeting.

I thought everybody took naps on Sunday afternoon for the modern-day equivalent of observing the Sabbath. I thought everybody knew that it was wrong to drink, smoke, cuss, go to movies, or dance. People who did those kinds of things were sinners, and they knew those things were sin just like we did.

I can still remember learning from some of my friends at the public school I attended that my family wasn't as normal as I thought it was. In fact, they thought my family was kind of strange. But then, I thought their families seemed strange too. I assumed that the way we lived our life was the correct way to live.

John Westerhoff describes several stages of faith development that we all go through on the way to arriving at what he calls "owned faith," the final or most mature stage of faith development. For almost everyone, that journey of faith begins with "experienced faith," the faith that we learn from the family culture that is experienced in the home.[27]

> FAMILY TRADITIONS
> ❧ FAMILY BIRTHDAYS ❧
>
> Whenever someone in your family has a birthday, make the dinnertime celebration special. Let the birthday person choose his or her favorite dish, then everyone except the birthday person helps prepare the meal. Give the birthday person a special place setting with a place of honor (if you have one). Have each person in the family say a prayer of blessing for the birthday person or share one thing they love or appreciate about him or her.

In fact, they thought my family was kind of strange. But then, I thought their families seemed strange too. I assumed that the way we lived our life was the correct way to live.

What is your family culture like? Let me say here that there is no family culture that is "right" or "best." Even among evangelical Christian families, each will have its own unique family culture. Tim Stafford writes:

When two people get married, they pick a little of the husband's family culture, a little of the wife's. They throw in something from the neighbors. They add their hobbies and interests, their personalities and ideals. They are influenced by what they admire on TV and the movies, and also by what region of the country they live in. . . . Stir all the various factors together, and you create the unique flavor that sets [your family] apart from every other family.[28]

The family culture that my wife and I created for our children is unlike all other families. We didn't deliberately try to be odd, but that's just how it turned out. We did life together based on our values, our interests, our obligations, and our priorities. Because I'm a banjo player and have played in several bluegrass bands, we've always had a lot of music in our home, and family vacations have frequently involved renting a motor home and traveling to a bluegrass music festival. Because I had been in youth ministry for so long, we almost always had teenagers around the house. We were constantly going to youth camps, conferences, and mission trips. My ministry as a writer and speaker meant that I frequently traveled away from home and sometimes took the whole family with me to faraway places, even to other countries. Because Marci and I were very involved as leaders in several small churches, we became close friends with many other couples whose children also became close friends with our children. It's unlikely that your family culture is anything at all like that

---

FAMILY TRADITIONS

❧ FAMILY MUSICAL FUN ❧

If your family likes music, get everyone a musical instrument they can learn to play together. I sometimes joke that "the family who picks together sticks together," and I've found it to be somewhat true. My two brothers, my sister, and I learned to play various folk instruments (guitar, banjo, mandolin, violin) when we were young and have had many opportunities to use our musical abilities, not only to entertain others but also to make our family get-togethers a lot of fun.

You may not think you (or your children) have musical talents, but you'll never really know unless you try. Music can be a fantastic activity to share together with your family. If your kids love to sing, invest in a karaoke machine. If they like the music they hear on the radio, buy one of those Guitar Hero video games so that you can get them more involved in music. Christian music tracks are available for both karaoke and Guitar Hero video games if you want them.

of my family, but I guarantee you that your family culture has had—or will have—a big impact on the faith journeys of your children.

Children can learn powerful lessons about God and about living the Christian life just from being a participant in your family life. That's why, when God gave the Israelites their religious faith—and the commandments—he also gave them numerous ways to pass that faith on from one generation to the next. Those ways made up the various family cultures within the nation of Israel, and the collective culture included all kinds of symbols and activities—bringing sacrifices to the temple, eating or not eating certain foods, celebrating various feasts and festivals. All of these practices were designed to remind the Israelites of who they were and what they believed; words alone would not suffice. If you've ever celebrated a Seder dinner (either Jewish or Christian), you know that this wonderful Passover tradition always involves the children. As you wash hands, break the matzo, taste the bitter herbs, and read the Old Testament verses, children act out the story of God's deliverance and ask the same questions that are always answered the same way by the elders. This was how the Jews taught their children the stories and lessons from their faith tradition, which they could then carry on to the next generation.

Children can learn powerful lessons about God and about living the Christian life just from being a participant in your family life.

You can also create a family culture that involves your children and communicates to them the values, priorities, and content of your faith in Jesus Christ. What you want to do is find some ways to live your family life so that your children will learn what it means to be a follower of Jesus in a natural and authentic way. My suggestion is that you not create your family culture just "for the kids" but because you believe these things are important in their own right and worth doing. Again, how you do this may be different from every other Christian family. In the rest of this chapter, I'll suggest a few ways that that have proven to be very effective for many families, including my own.

family devotions

In generations past, it was common—even expected—for Christian families to have a time of family devotions every day. Such devotions are a regularly scheduled time for family Bible reading and prayer. When I was very young, I remember my parents reading from the Bible at the breakfast table every morning, or from a popular devotional guide. This was a normal part of our particular family culture and I assumed that everybody started their day this way. Family devotions were just as much a part of my breakfast as was a bowl of my favorite sugarcoated cereal.

HOLIDAY CELEBRATIONS
❧ SEDER DINNER ❧

On the Thursday before Easter (Maundy Thursday), invite a few friends and family to gather for a Seder Dinner. A Seder is especially suited for teaching children because a traditional Seder service involves the children in asking questions and participating in the ritual drama, which is simple but powerful.

The Seder is the Passover meal, the Last Supper, which Jesus and his disciples ate on the night he was betrayed. Even if you're not Jewish, you'll find the service to be quite meaningful, a special way to celebrate Easter week. There are resources available online, or you can visit a local synagogue to purchase the supplies that you'll need. A Passover Seder for Christians also can be found online if you search on the Internet.

Later on, when I was a teenager, we didn't have family devotions as often as we did when I was a child, probably because family schedules starting getting crazy. We'd miss a couple of days and then realize we hadn't had devotions in a week or two. I'm sure my parents felt guilty about this because having family devotions was preached from the pulpit and expected of all true Christian families.

Today, you don't hear as much about family devotions, even from the pulpit. I conducted a parenting seminar a couple of years ago at a large Southern California church and asked the audience, "How many of you have family devotions with your children?" Two or three hands went up, but mostly I got blank looks from around the room. One parent raised his hand and asked, "What are family devotions?" He really wanted to know.

You don't find too many parents who conduct family devotions the same way parents did several generations ago. We no longer live in small towns or on farms where life is predictable and routine. Few families today have schedules similar to those of earlier generations, when everyone went to school at the same time and came home from work at the same time. As David Elkind writes in his book *Ties That Stress*:

> . . . [today's] home is no longer a haven, a place for nurturance and protection. Rather it is more like a railway station, with parents and children pulling in and out as they go about their busy lives. In many homes, family meals are a relic [of the past]. In middle-class homes, one parent comes home late from the office while the other parent is driving one or more children to piano lessons or scouts. In other homes one or both parents may be working a shift at the usual meal times.[29]

One parent raised his hand and asked, "What are family devotions?" He really wanted to know.

It's completely understandable why parents today are resistant to the idea of having regular family devotions. Doing so will take a commitment that's going to be difficult to begin (if you've never or rarely done them), to maintain, and to do well. If holding family devotions means gathering the entire family together at a regular time and place for daily Bible reading and prayer, it's probably not going to happen for most families. For these reasons, the old standard of daily devotions may be unrealistic for many families, but weekly or twice-weekly devotions should not be. And then there's the perception—or maybe I should say misperception—thing. If the picture of family devotions you have in your head looks like something out of *Ozzie and Harriet,* with the kids and mom sitting quietly at dad's feet as he drones on and on, I wouldn't blame you if your first thought is "thanks but no thanks" to trying *that.*

The key to successful family devotions today is to avoid doing them out of a sense of obligation or anxiety or guilt and instead making sure they're done from a sincere desire to lead your children to walk with God.

So are family devotions still a good idea? Absolutely. They may not look exactly the same as they did a generation or two ago, but they can still be an effective way for parents to have regular faith conversations with their children and to be the spiritual leaders in their families that God intended them to be. Family devotions can become part of your family culture and something that helps set your family apart from all others. They can become a focal point of your family life and provide you with the opportunities you need to intentionally pass your faith on to your kids.

The key to successful family devotions today is to avoid doing them out of a sense of obligation or anxiety or guilt and instead making sure they're done from a sincere desire to lead your children to walk with God. They don't have to be forced—and indeed, shouldn't be—or just one more activity to add to an already busy family calendar. They don't have to be boring lectures or discussions that end with awkward and embarrassing silences. In fact, they don't even have to be called family devotions. You can call them Power Hour or Family Fun Time or Jesus Chat or any other name that fits your family. One family I know calls theirs Roundup Time (yes, they are into horses). The important thing is that you make them a priority. Even with the busy lifestyles that nearly everyone has today, we can still make time for things that are important to us. Don't let the church, the school, the job, or the entertainment industry set the agenda for your family. If you have meetings every night of the week, cancel some of them so that you can free up the time you need to be with your kids, instructing them in God's Word and teaching them what it means to be a follower of Jesus. If you've made the Joshua commitment ("As for me and my household, we will worship the Lord!"), then this is not something you'll find difficult or unreasonable to do.

Here are a few other suggestions for making family devotions work for you.

First, don't over-commit. Begin with a schedule that fits your family. It could be once a week, once a month, twice a week, twice a month—there's no one way to do it. A regular time—that repeats on a weekly or monthly basis—is probably the best plan simply because everyone can put it on their calendars in advance. Don't assume that you'll find time on the fly. Select a good time when you know your family can meet, and then make sure everyone agrees to it and looks forward to the time.

Combine your time of family devotions with family fun. Before or after your devotions, you might want to play games together, watch a video, ride bikes, or eat ice cream sundaes.

If you have meetings every night of the week, cancel some of them so that you can free up the time you need to be with your kids, instructing them in God's Word and teaching them what it means to be a follower of Jesus.

Change things up. Avoid boredom; make sure you don't do the same things over and over. If the weather is nice, get out of the house. Have devotions in different places in the house, and not the same place every time.

Keep it short. Rambling on and on is not an effective way to keep the attention of your kids. Usually one good point is enough. Get to it right away. If you spend just twenty minutes a week (about three minutes a day!) intentionally teaching your children about the things of God from the time they are four years old until they're fifteen, they'll have received nearly two hundred hours of spiritual training from you. That's a significant amount of time, especially when you consider that parents have more influence on children than anyone else.

Be creative. Remember that your kids learn in a variety of ways. Use object lessons, stories, illustrations, skits, and anything you can think of to enhance your teaching. Take advantage of the many resources that are available to you so that you can change things up and do things differently from time to time.

Avoid lecturing. Remember, your kids are part of a generation whose attention spans were formed by watching TV, using computers, and playing video games. They need to be active rather than passive participants. Here's an example: ask your children to do a quick search around the house for objects that remind them of God's blessings or God's love. In five minutes, see who can bring back the most items. Then talk about them. Bottom line: just be creative and get the kids involved.

Use humor and fun. Not all devotions have to be serious. If you have fun with your kids while you're teaching, you'll create some wonderful memories for them. If you're teaching the story of David and Goliath, play the role of Goliath and let your kids see if they can hit you in the head with five smooth stones (marshmallows, of course). If you're teaching Noah and the ark to smaller children, get a toy boat, some plastic animals, put 'em in the bathtub, and make a movie with your kids doing the narration. Try that and see if your kids aren't howling with laughter!

Get the whole family involved, *especially* the children. Let the kids pick out a topic they're interested in or have everyone place topics in a paper bag and draw one out for the next devotion. If kids have a say in what they're learning, they'll be more apt to pay attention and participate.

Incorporate real life lessons. While reading from the Bible about a particular event and the lesson it provides, show your family how you've applied this lesson to your life. Go around the room and offer anyone who has had similar experiences to share with the family. Make the devotion real.

If kids have a say in what they're learning, they'll
be more apt to pay attention and participate.

Don't try to be something or someone you're not. Be real. Let your kids get inside both your head and heart. When you are open and honest with them, they will look forward to these special times with you.

I've scattered numerous family devotion ideas throughout this book. Don't be afraid to give family devotions a try in your home and don't be discouraged if they don't go quite they way you had hoped. You may get plenty of "devotion commotion." Just don't give up on what you're doing. Keep trying different things and I guarantee that your children will be grateful to you later on even if they don't seem very grateful right now. Start slow with something short you can do on a daily or weekly basis or just by taking a few minutes before or after dinner. Or perhaps simply pray at bedtime to get started, or read from the Bible at that time. It really doesn't matter so much *what* you do as long as you intentionally take the time to *do it*. Use and adapt the various ideas in this book; try different approaches to see what works best for you and your family.

family traditions

Another important way to create a family culture in which children can learn about God and how to live the Christian faith is through family traditions. (Again, I've sprinkled these throughout the book, and a list of holiday ideas follows in the latter half of this chapter.) Family traditions can provide wonderful opportunities for you to pass on your faith and values to your children. There are many kinds of family traditions. Some are spiritual in nature, like praying before meals. Some traditions come from your family's cultural or ethnic heritage, like eating Tennessee smoked sausage, having biscuits and gravy on Christmas morning (one of ours), or something as eclectic as going to the Scottish games every year. Some traditions aren't very traditional. For example, one of ours is that we almost never eat dinner at the dinner table on Monday nights from September through December. We get TV trays and eat in the family room because we watch *Monday Night Football*, which comes on during the dinner hour on the West Coast (and the TV is in the family room, not in the kitchen or dining room). OK, I admit this is not a tradition I would recommend to others, but it's a tradition we continue to this day because we're big football fans.

Traditions are the "we always" of families, like "We always make snow ice cream at the first snowfall" or "We always have games and popcorn on Saturday night."

Even when family traditions are just for fun (like our habit of taking a picture of our family in the exact same pose in front of the Christmas tree every year) they help to make the connection between family members and sometimes between generations. Traditions are the "we always" of families, like "We always make snow ice cream at the first snowfall" or "We always have games and popcorn on Saturday night." The habit of praying before mealtimes or reciting the Lord's Prayer together at bedtime or making sure there is a cross displayed in every room of the house are traditions that create feelings of warmth and closeness, a sense of belonging and family identity. They also promote a feeling of safety and security within the family by providing predictable and familiar experiences. Family members have something to look forward to that gives them a sense of assurance in a hectic and ever-changing world. Even as today's families suffer from busy lifestyles, they can stay connected by being intentional about maintaining important rituals and traditions. I'm always amazed that our grown children still want to come home to participate in some of the traditions we've established over the years.

For the past twenty-five years or so our family has hosted a backyard Easter celebration that has become a tradition not only for us but also for about a hundred of our friends. Living in Southern California, we almost always have perfect spring weather (we had rain only one year that I can remember), so we spruce up the backyard with lots of flowers and Easter decorations. We have a potluck meal, egg hunts for the kids, and bluegrass music performed by my band and many of my musician friends. It's an exhilarating and fun day that's focused entirely on the Easter event—the resurrection of Jesus. We've always believed that the resurrection is the centerpiece of the Christian faith and we've chosen to make it the centerpiece of our family as well. In fact, we start our Easter celebration well before Easter by observing Ash Wednesday as well as the Lenten season. We attend Good Friday services and sometimes a Seder (Passover) meal on Maundy Thursday. Not all families go all out celebrating Easter the way we do, but we've chosen to celebrate Easter the way many families celebrate Christmas. This is what we always do, and it expresses a good deal of who we are and what we believe.

Most family traditions establish themselves just by repetition. In the case of our Easter celebration, we never intended to do it every year. But everyone enjoyed the first one so much that we did it again the following year and the year after that. Now we can't imagine Easter any other way. It has become a tradition, our way of doing Easter, which connects us to our faith, to each other, and to many other people as well.

Holidays are an ideal time for establishing family traditions because they come around once every year. Whether it's decorating Easter eggs, going to the same spot together to watch the Fourth of July fireworks, making Christmas cookies, or finding the same spot on the sidewalk for the Tournament of Roses parade on New Year's Day, take advantage of those recurring opportunities to create traditions that provide your children with a sense of expectation and a strong connection to your family's identity. It's a short leap from there to your family's collective identity as followers of Jesus.

You can adapt the sampling of holiday tradition ideas in this chapter, and I'll have a few more in the final chapter of this book.

Don't worry if you don't have too many family traditions. You don't want to have so many that they seem burdensome or cause family members to feel a bit weird. Your goal should be to keep traditions in your family that serve a useful purpose, make a positive contribution to the family culture, and affirm each member of the family. You don't want to keep family traditions going that aren't worth keeping.

HOLIDAY CELEBRATIONS
EASTER SUNRISE SERVICE

Yes, it's really early in the morning, but getting the family up on Easter morning to attend an Easter sunrise service can be a wonderful family tradition. Don't just drag your kids out of bed to this service without first teaching them the significance and meaning of the event. Build their anticipation for it with their Easter baskets and it can be just as exciting as Christmas morning.

HOLIDAY CELEBRATIONS
TIME LAPSE PHOTOGRAPHY

Make a special ritual of decorating the Christmas tree every year and then take a photo of the family in front of the decorated tree—in exactly the same pose. Begin when the children are very young and these pictures will make a nice scrapbook when your kids are older.

HOLIDAY CELEBRATIONS
ADVENT CALENDARS

Buy or make an advent calendar for the Christmas season and light advent candles each night as you count down the days until Christmas. You can find resources and ideas on the Web or in a store that sells Christian supplies. This is a fantastic way to keep the holiday season focused on the true meaning of Christmas.

Let me add here that having dinner together as a family is one of the easiest and most important traditions you can establish. I'm always amazed by how many people no longer have time for dinner around a real dinner table with real plates and place settings. (For some people, cleaning up after dinner is collecting all the fast-food trash out of the back of their car.) Even if it isn't home-cooked, eating dinner together with your family on a regular basis can have many benefits besides just making sure everybody gets a square meal once a day. Researchers have found that children and teenagers who have frequent fam-

ily dinners with their parents (at least five per week) are much less likely to engage in harmful behaviors like smoking and substance abuse.[30] I realize that job schedules or other obligations (like watching *Monday Night Football*) may prevent some families from eating dinner together in the traditional way every night, but if you can do it, this is, without any question, worth the effort. Make dinnertime a nonnegotiable part of your family's daily routine and do your best to make it a positive experience for everyone.

family service

When children regularly participate in acts of missions and service together with their parents, there is a much greater likelihood that those children will come to adopt the values and faith of their parents as well. The call to follow Jesus is the call to serve, and when children are given the opportunity to serve while they are young, they'll be drawn to service for the rest of their lives.

I have a friend in Chicago who takes his son to a downtown park every Sunday morning to serve donuts and coffee to homeless people. They do it every week in all kinds of weather all year long. It has become their ministry together and neither would miss doing it for the world. They've made friends with homeless people they see every week and have had a chance to share their faith in Christ with many of them.

You may not want to take your children to your downtown to minister to the homeless. It's natural for parents to want to protect their children from the harsher realities of life. But if you really want your children to develop a heart for God and a heart for those whom Christ called "the least of these" and "brothers of mine" (Matthew 25:40), you'll want to get them out of their comfort zones from time to time. You can serve in a soup kitchen, a mental health facility, or visit the elderly in a nursing home. You don't have to go far from home to perform meaningful acts of missions and service.

HOLIDAY CELEBRATIONS

❧ CHRISTMAS LETTERS, SONGS, AND GIFTS FOR JESUS ❧

Before opening your Christmas presents, have everyone in your family write a thank you letter to Jesus. Collect them and bring them out every Christmas. Keep adding new letters annually. To make the tradition work even better, add this rule: family members can only read the thank you letters they have written.

Still more to do on Christmas morning: when you're having your normal Christmas Day celebration, sing "Happy Birthday" to Jesus as a way to remind everyone whose birthday you're celebrating. Children are very familiar with the song and sometimes it communicates the meaning of Christmas even better than many Christmas carols.

To add even more meaning to this birthday party, have everyone bring one gift for Jesus that will be given to the poor (which, of course, is the same thing as giving a gift to Jesus).

For quite a few years my wife and I regularly took our family across the border to help with a local San Diego missions organization serving poor migrant families who were living around the dump in Tijuana, Mexico. The first few times we went it was quite scary and uncomfortable, but as we continued to go on a monthly basis, our children began to look forward to the experience. As a family, we started our own little ministry and called it Operation Cinderella. We would purchase children's shoes at a discount on our side of the border and then take them to the Tijuana dump and look for children who had no shoes. Children would line up at our van and we would wash the feet of the children and then match their feet with a new pair of shoes. As we went back months later, we often found children still wearing those shoes that we gave them in the name of Jesus.

Many churches and missions organizations organize mission trips to Mexico or other poor countries to help build houses, conduct Vacation Bible School programs, or assist in medical clinics. Some families make these trips part of their family vacations. A trip like this can require a major commitment as money, time, and a lot of discomfort is often involved. But it can be a life-changing experience for kids as well. Every year my wife and I accompany our youth group to Mexico for a week of service, and while we know we can't change Mexico, we do see a lot of change take place in the lives of the young people who go on the trip. Last summer I accompanied a group of families to Mexico to help them build houses for the poor, and many of the parents told me afterward that they plan to do this every year. The experience they had with their kids was well worth the expense—which was considerable because some had to travel two thousand miles to get there—and the difficult conditions that they had to endure.

Closer to home, you can visit shut-ins or do chores for elderly people who live right down the street. You can do a trash walk through your neighborhood or "flower" somebody's house. I have a friend who is a landscaper and when he hears about someone going through a difficult time, he and his family anonymously plant beautiful flowers in the beds of that person's front yard. They usually do this secretly when the person is away from home just to bring a little joy (and a lot of color!) into their lives. I know because I was the recipient of this amazing gift when my wife was in the hospital a few years ago.

HOLIDAY CELEBRATIONS

❧ SECRET SANTA ❧

As a family, select one person you know who is lonely, needy, or just needs encouragement. Purchase or create a special gift for this person. Then on Christmas Eve or Christmas morning, get the family out of bed, bundle up, grab some cookies and hot cocoa, pile into the family vehicle, and drive the gift over to the person's home. Sneak the gift onto the front porch and include an attached card that reads "From your Secret Santa." (And there are many ways to vary this idea through the season, of course.)

One of the ways our family has been involved in missions and service over the years has been by sponsoring a child through Compassion International. There are many missions organizations that make it possible to do this, but we've always been impressed with the good work that Compassion does to help children in third world countries. Compassion partners with local churches and missions to provide Christian education, health care, nutrition, and job training for children who otherwise could never afford to get those things. For years, our family has sponsored one or more children, and through letter writing and some face-to-face visits we've learned that we make a huge difference in the lives of these children and families. From an experience like this, your child will learn more about following Jesus than you could ever teach them through a thousand sermons and lectures.

> **HOLIDAY CELEBRATIONS**
>
> ### ❧ STILL MORE CHRISTMAS CELEBRATION IDEAS ❧
>
> - Visit a nursing home with your family. There are usually quite a few lonely people living in nursing homes who really appreciate having their spirits lifted. Sing a few Christmas carols and leave some homemade cookies. It's a great way to share the love of Jesus with sick and elderly people.
> - Hold a family Christmas pageant: act out the Christmas story with your kids.
> - Go Christmas caroling as a family and give a small gift to the people you visit.
> - Find the neighborhoods in your town that go over the top with Christmas lights and drive around looking at them. If you really want to get crazy, have everyone dress in their pajamas, take popcorn, and turn up the Christmas tunes while you drive!

If you'd like to explore more ideas and resources for family missions and service, let me recommend a great book: *The Busy Family's Guide to Volunteering: Doing Good Together*, by Jenny Friedman (Beltsville, Maryland: Robins Lane Press, 2003).

family fun

Something I've noticed over the years in working with youth and families is that families who laugh together easily are also families who seem to worship and pray together easily. I've come to believe that families who have fun together are also families with a strong sense of family unity, shared values, and shared faith. I've often wondered if this is a chicken-or-egg situation. Do healthy families laugh more or does laughter produce healthy families? Early on in our marriage, my wife and I decided not to leave that to chance. We tried to keep the laughter flowing in our home. I believe that family fun is one of the best ways to communicate to children some important attributes of the Christian faith, like joy, grace, and gratitude. When you can laugh with your kids and celebrate their lives with them now, it opens the door for the kind of laughter and celebrating that we'll all be doing someday in Heaven. I'm convinced that children are more likely to be drawn to Christ and to the family of God when they experience joy and laughter in the homes where they live.

HOLIDAY CELEBRATIONS

꽃 THANKSGIVING AT A HOMELESS SHELTER 꽃

One great way to teach your children that it is more blessed to give than to receive is to volunteer to serve meals at a homeless shelter or rescue mission on Thanksgiving Day. Some families do this on alternating years—a traditional family Thanksgiving dinner at home on, say, the odd-numbered years, and serving Thanksgiving dinner at a homeless shelter on the even-numbered years.

FAMILY SERVICE

꽃 CARE PACKAGES 꽃

As a family service project, prepare a few care packages to keep in your car so that you'll have them available when you encounter homeless people or others in need. Packages can include basic toiletry and food items and perhaps a copy of the New Testament.

Once again, I've tried to include plenty of family fun ideas throughout this book. Every family can have fun in their own way, of course. What's fun to one family may seem boring, odd, or impossible to others. But here are a few fun things that most children love to do with their parents.

Play games with your kids. Maybe you can set aside one night of the week or month to have a Boggle, Clue, or Yahtzee tournament. There are all kinds of old board games (Monopoly, checkers anyone?) that many children never play these days because so many of their games are electronic. Invent your own games. Play old favorites like hide-and-seek or hopscotch. The more you play with your children, the more opportunities you'll have to share God's love with them. With older children, find a sport or activity they enjoy and participate in it with them. Shoot hoops, play tennis or racquetball, challenge them to a game of chess. To borrow a phrase, families that spend time playing together are much more likely to spend time praying together.

Celebrate anything good that happens in your family. Put together a "fun closet" full of games, costumes, party supplies, sparkling cider, and the like and keep all this handy for any occasion. You never know when you'll have a need to throw a quick party.

Take a family portrait of everyone dressed up in funny clothes. Go to a thrift store and see if you can dress up as a family of nerds or hillbillies or as a heavy metal rock band. Then use that picture for your next Christmas card.

Laughter and play open the door to warmth and closeness in a family. Whenever you have a smile on your face, you are communicating affection and affirmation to other members of the family.

Play harmless practical jokes on each other from time to time. As long as they're not mean-spirited, these can be funny and affirming. Secretly fill your kid's bedroom full of balloons from floor to ceiling. Put clear plastic wrap under the toilet seat or petroleum jelly on top of it. Put the same sort of stuff on their doorknobs. Load their toothbrushes with salt. Put marbles in the medicine cabinet. Short-sheet a bed. Serve mashed potato sundaes. Make fake candies by dipping squares of soap in chocolate. Wake your kids up in the morning wearing a gorilla costume. And be sure to take videos! OK, don't do all of these things on the same day or you'll traumatize your poor kids! But with discretion, a few tasteful and well-executed practical jokes can be a fun way to keep the laughter flowing in your home.

Still more ways to have fun together:

- Watch old family videos together.
- Have a family movie night watching classic comedies.
- Camp out overnight in the backyard.
- Put together a giant puzzle with your family.

Remember that the reason for doing things like these is just to have fun with your family. Laughter and play open the door to warmth and closeness in a family. Whenever you have a smile on your face, you are communicating affection and affirmation to other members of the family. I've been in many Christian homes that were not characterized by joy, but instead were marked by negativity, stress, anxiety, and fear. Many years ago I heard a preacher say, "If you love God . . . If you're grateful that he sent his Son to die on the cross for your sins . . . If you have experienced the joy of knowing and serving Christ . . . then please, notify your face!" The joy of the Christian life comes not from just doing things but from being able to laugh and have fun together even in times of difficulty and trouble—because we know that Christ is with us and that God is always in control.

QUESTIONS FOR REFLECTION
AND ACTION

1 || Rank the following methods from 1 (not good) to 10 (great!), as you see them, for parents to pass their faith on to their kids.

___ Homeschooling your children
___ Holding family devotions on a regular basis
___ Hiring a tutor who's a Christian
___ Giving your children Christian books to read
___ Making them attend church every week
___ Letting them figure out spiritual things entirely for themselves
___ Keeping them away from worldly influences
___ Threatening them with a loss of privileges or their inheritance
___ Praying for them every day
___ Sending them to a private Christian school

2 || When are the best times for you to have faith conversations with your children?

When is the last time you had a faith conversation with your children? How did it go?

3 How do your children learn best? List some reasons why you think so.

- Hearing _____
- Seeing _____
- Doing _____

4 On a scale of 1 to 10, how would you rate the importance of having regular family devotions for the purpose of helping your children grow spiritually? Why?

Not at all 1   2   3   4   5   6   7   8   9   10 **Very important**

5 List some of your family activities that have helped contribute to your child's/children's faith development. How did they do so?

- Family fun
- Family service
- Family traditions

community

J"Joe, do you know where our son is?"

"You mean Jesus? Isn't he with you?"

"I haven't seen him since we left Jerusalem!"

"Didn't he go on that Holy City sightseeing tour with you while I was getting our tents repaired?"

"No, he didn't. But he knew to be back at the East Gate by sundown."

"Have you checked with James, Uncle Zach, or Elizabeth?"

"They haven't seen hide nor hair of him since yesterday morning, Joseph! Where on earth do you think he could be? I'm so worried . . . he might have been kidnapped by Samaritans!"

"Let's not fear the worst, Mary. First, let's make sure he's not with the rest of the family or with friends. If he's not with any of them, then we'll just turn our donkeys around and head back to Jerusalem. Don't worry. . . . We'll find him."

And they did, of course—three days later! While we have very little information about the childhood of Jesus, Luke records this incredible story in his Gospel account (Luke 2:41-50) probably because it was a favorite of Jesus' disciples. *"Hey Simon, did Jesus ever tell you about the time his mom and dad left him behind in Jerusalem? He was only twelve years old at the time!"*

I can certainly identify with Mary and Joseph. One year I lost my 8-year-old daughter, Amber, at the Los Angeles County Fair. I was there performing with my bluegrass band and she somehow wandered off and went missing for more than an hour—which still ranks right up there as one of the most terrifying hours of my life. We eventually found her sucking on a lollipop at the "lost parent" booth.

Sometimes we misunderstand the complementary roles that parents and the community play in the upbringing of children. Parents usually err in one of two ways.

Many have wondered how Mary and Joseph could possibly have made such a horrible mistake. Today they would certainly have called 911 and the story would have been all over the evening news. *"Son of God missing for three days! Video at eleven!"* We don't know the extent of Mary and Joseph's anxiety during this time, but Luke tells us the parents assumed Jesus "was in their company" (v. 44), which doesn't necessarily mean they expected him to be tagging along right beside them but rather somewhere in their traveling party, in their *community*. In those days, when families made the long journey to Jerusalem, especially for Passover, they typically traveled with their entire household, including grandparents, uncles, aunts, cousins, employees, and the like. Historians say that a typical traveling family in Bible times may have numbered as many as sixty people! When Mary and Joseph lost track of Jesus, they went looking for him first among their family and friends because it really wasn't all that unusual for children to spend long periods of time with caring adults who were part of their extended family.

Some of us are old enough to remember when we had communities like that. As a child I could wander off during the day and spend hours at the home of one of my friends down the street or playing with friends in the nearby lemon orchard or public park a few blocks from my home. I honestly don't think my parents ever seriously worried about my safety. I can still remember the names of many of the neighbors who knew me as a child, and most of them certainly would have come to the rescue if they had noticed I was in any trouble, or would have disciplined me if I caused any. But few of us live in Mayberry these days, and as M. Scott Peck wrote as the opening line in his book *The Different Drum*, "Community is currently rare."[31]

The point of this chapter is really quite simple. Parents were never meant to raise children in the faith all by themselves. As the old African proverb puts it (or was it Hillary Clinton?): "It takes a village." The Bible agrees with that idea and it's almost a wonder that Moses or Solomon or some other Biblical writer didn't say it exactly the same way. While the Deuteronomy 6 commission was given first of all to parents, it was addressed to the entire faith community. *"Hear, O Israel,"* the Israelites were admonished in consecutive sentences (Deuteronomy 6:3, 4). No one was exempt from teaching the commandments of God to the generations behind them just because they didn't have any kids. We are all part of the family of God and all of us have a role to play in the spiritual training of every one of our children.

Sometimes we misunderstand the complementary roles that parents and the community play in the upbringing of children. Parents usually err in one of two ways. The first we've mentioned several times already in this book, and that's the tendency of some parents to outsource the spiritual training of their children to somebody else. But the other mistake is equally dangerous. That's when parents try to isolate their kids from other people so that they won't be negatively influenced. Not only is this virtually impossible to do in today's world, sooner or later the isolationist approach backfires when children have to transition themselves into the real world and leave behind the artificial world their parents created for them at home.

There's a better way, and that's what I call circling the wagons. In other words, we simply need to surround our children with as many good people as we can find. While we will always be the most important influencers of our children, we need other voices speaking into their lives that can validate and reinforce the values and spiritual training that we give our children at home.

I sometimes compare the effect that other caring adults have in the lives of our kids with epoxy glue. Do you know what epoxy is? I always keep plenty of it in my garage. Whenever anything breaks, I usually go straight for the epoxy. It's stronger than any other glue on the market, I'm sure. The interesting concept behind epoxy is that it really doesn't exist until you create it. You buy a kind of epoxy kit that consists of two tubes of gooey stuff. One is a light-colored goo called resin and the other is a dark-colored stuff called hardener. When you mix them together, you get a chemical reaction that turns the combined gooeyness into a substance that will soon

> **FAMILY TRADITIONS**
> **❧ UNIQUE FAMILY HOLIDAYS ❧**
>
> Your family may celebrate Christmas, Thanksgiving, or the Fourth of July, but what about Kids Day? Never heard of it? No problem. You can create your own Kids Day on any day of the year you want, maybe on the day that falls exactly halfway between Mother's Day and Father's Day. Another idea: if your family has a special religious or historical figure everyone admires (like C.S. Lewis, Martin Luther, William Wilberforce, or any of a number of others), make that person's birthday an annual celebration in your home. Invent your own way of celebrating your special holiday and make it an annual fun family tradition.

become hard as steel. I admit I'm not a rocket scientist, so I'm always kind of amazed at how you can combine two elements—which by themselves don't stick to anything—and get something else entirely, a substance that's one of the world's strongest bonding agents. I've used it to fix motors, musical instruments, bicycles, bricks, even fishing poles.

There's no question that you as a parent are the most powerful and decisive influence on the spiritual lives of your children, but don't ever think for a minute that you will be able to bond them to Christ and his church all by yourself. You need the "hardener" of a caring community of like-minded believers who can provide you with support and encouragement along the way. As Paul wrote to the church at Galatia, "Carry each other's burdens, and in this way you will fulfill the law of Christ" (Galatians 6:2).

Let's walk through just a few of the places where you will find that kind of community.

grandparents

One of the first places to look for support in your parenting role is to your immediate family. Grandparents (as well as other members of your extended family) can play a vital role in the faith development of your children. Scripture repeatedly includes grandparents in the formula for passing on faith to the next generation. "Only be careful, and watch yourselves closely so that you do not forget the things your eyes have seen or let them slip from your heart as long as you live. Teach them to your children and to their children after them" (Deuteronomy 4:9).

While we will always be the most important influencers of our children, we need other voices speaking into their lives that can validate and reinforce the values and spiritual training that we give our children at home.

The apostle Paul begins his second letter to Timothy by reminding his young disciple of the background and heritage of his family. "I have been reminded of your sincere faith, which first lived in your grandmother Lois and in your mother Eunice and, I am persuaded, now lives in you also" (2 Timothy 1:5). Here Paul encourages Timothy to continue imitating the examples of these godly women who lived devout lives in the middle of a pagan culture.

It's tempting to assume that biblical families were much less complicated and more stable than families are in today's postmodern world. But families have always required great effort to keep together and to remain functioning in a healthy and supportive way. We don't know all the details of young Timothy's life, but we do know that he was the product of a mixed marriage—a Greek father and a mother who was a believing Jew. Some scholars suspect that Eunice might have been a single parent, perhaps due to religious incompatibilities. All we know for certain is that Paul doesn't mention anything about Timothy's father or refer to his example in this letter.

Families were fragile in Bible times and they are no less fragile today. Perhaps that's why God in his wisdom ordained that every child should have at least six adults (if both sets of grandparents are around) to provide love and care for them and to make sure faith gets passed from one generation to the next.

It's tempting to assume that biblical families were much less complicated and more stable than families are in today's postmodern world. But families have always required great effort to keep together and to remain functioning in a healthy and supportive way.

Recently I had a conversation with a single mom at one of my parenting seminars. She was worried that she would not be able to train her children up in the faith because her ex-husband, who takes care of the kids on weekends, is not a believer. I encouraged her, first of all, not to underestimate the incredible amount of influence that she herself could have on her children. When I inquired a little further about her family, she told me that her parents, who were also believers, lived only a few minutes away. The rest of my advice to her was a no-brainer: let those children spend as much time as possible with grandma and grandpa, if the grandparents are willing and able. See if there isn't some way you can arrange schedules so that those grandparents can love on their grandchildren more often. A godly mother plus the love of godly grandparents equals more than enough influence for God to use in a powerful way.

In the past, grandparents had lots of grandchildren; today, kids have a lot of grandparents. With the rise of blended families, adoptive families, foster families, and the like, children can easily have four parents and eight or more grandparents. If your children's grandparents are accessible, willing, and able to come alongside their grandkids in a positive and supportive way, this can be a tremendous asset and advantage for the kids. Loving grandparents have always played a significant role in the lives of children, but today they are more important than ever.

Researchers have found that grandparents rank just behind the influence of mom (number one) and dad (number two) as the primary religious influencers of children, and they rank significantly *ahead* of friends, pastors, entertainers, youth group leaders, and just about every other influence you can name.[32] Grandparents bring many of the same assets to the table as parents do, but they additionally provide some experience-based wisdom that is missing today in the lives of many young people. Our children are growing up in a rapidly changing culture that has little time for reflection, no roots, no perspective, and little history. Words like *commitment, sacrifice, fidelity, discipline,* and *authority* are out of fashion and largely unknown to many young people today because they have no relevance and seem so inconvenient. But grandparents not only have memories of these words, they appreciate their significance for a life well lived. This is especially true for older generations that have walked faithfully with God down through the years. Jay Kesler, in his book *Grandparenting*, writes:

> The world is changing rapidly—too fast perhaps, and in the wrong directions. . . . Young people need something stable to hang on to—a culture connection, a sense of their own past, a hope for their own future. Most of all, they need what grandparents can give them—a picture of the long-term faithfulness of God.[33]

At this writing, I have three grandchildren and one on the way. There's hardly anything I enjoy hearing more than "Come on, Grandpa, let's play!" As David put it in one of his psalms:

"Even when I am old and gray,

do not forsake me, O God,

till I declare your power to the next generation,

your might to all who are to come" (Psalm 71:18).

I consider it a great blessing that God has given me another generation to whom I can declare the power of God. I pray that I will be faithful to that calling and I know that other grandparents pray the same.

Maybe your children don't have grandparents available to them or those who are able to provide that kind of positive example or influence. There may be other members of your extended family or even someone else's family who could serve in a similar role. I know many children who have become very attached to older adults in their church or neighborhood who have adopted them as their spiritual grandchildren. When children have older adults who care about them and are willing to spend time with them, it's a wonderful and powerful gift from one generation to the next. Don't be afraid to seek out older and wiser adults who might be willing to come alongside your children in this very significant way.

the church

Certainly one place you may be able to find those kinds of adults—and many others who can contribute to the faith development of your children—is in your local church. The church can be a wonderful blessing to you and your family if you take advantage of it. New research by the Barna Group indicates that children and teenagers who attend church are much more likely to hold on to their faith when they become adults.[34]

Just remember that it's not the church's job to evangelize and disciple your kids. No pastor, no youth worker, no Sunday school teacher, no children's worker—no matter how gifted and well educated he or she might be—can hold a candle to *you* as the primary shaper of your children's faith. Parents who embrace the "dump and run strategy" of dropping their kids off at church while they run off until the allotted time has expired make a very serious mistake. It would actually be better if the children dropped these parents off at church so that they could be taught how to train up their children in the faith at home!

That said, the church is extremely important for your family's spiritual health. You need the church and the church needs you. If you want your children to grow up with a strong faith that will last, it's crucial that you stay committed to a local church and make church attendance a priority for your family. If you are not involved in a church while your children are at home, there is little chance that your children will be involved in a church when they leave home. And if they don't stay connected to the body of Christ, they are not likely to stay connected to the head—Jesus himself—either.

I consider it a great blessing that God has given me another generation to whom I can declare the power of God. I pray that I will be faithful to that calling and I know that other grandparents pray the same.

There is a growing trend among some young Christians to believe that you can be a follower of Jesus without being involved in his church. They advocate doing church at the local coffee shop or out on the golf course rather than meeting with a lot of boring people you don't like very much in a stuffy old church building.

I agree that the church—and the people in it—can at times be boring. But then, so are a lot of things that are really important to me, like my marriage and my job. Life isn't a constant roller-coaster ride. And there's no question that when you go to church you have to put up with some obnoxious people. I've discovered that the church is full of hypocrites and sinners, which is exactly what it's supposed to be full of. Those are the people Jesus died for on the cross—and I am one of them.

Despite all the problems that churches are famous for, almost every church I know does a lot of good things that individuals and families can't always do very well on their own. Churches take care of old people, bring meals to new moms, send people to help at the local rescue mission, support missionaries overseas, provide comfort for people who have lost loved ones, give money for disaster relief, help with shelter for the homeless, and do many more things. The church is not a glorified coffeehouse where you go to have a double latte with other like-minded Christians; it's a place to hear God's word proclaimed and affirmed, to sing praises to God, and to serve others in the name of Christ. It is a place where children are dedicated, believers are baptized, faith is confirmed, marriage vows are said, and the Holy Communion is celebrated.

Kevin DeYoung and Ted Kluck, authors of *Why We Love the Church* (Moody Publishers, 2009), write:

> The church is more than plural for Christian. It is both organism and organization, a living thing comprised of a certain order, regular worship services, with doctrinal standards, institutional norms, and defined rituals. Without the institution of the church nurturing the flock and protecting the faith for two thousand years, there would be no Christianity.[35]

Hebrews 10:25 says that we should not neglect "meeting together, as some are in the habit of doing, but let us encourage one another—and all the more as you see the Day approaching." It's indisputable that the early Christians, even under some difficult circumstances, regularly gathered to be more than just an invisible church. Whether it was in Jerusalem, Corinth, Philippi, or Rome, they worshipped together, prayed together, and risked their lives encouraging and equipping each other to take the gospel to the whole world.

❧ MORE HOLIDAY ACTIVITIES ❧

Here's another round of holiday ideas and activities for your family.

Un-Christmas cards and letters. If you're in the habit of sending out Christmas cards or Christmas letters each year, why not change things up and send out a Thanksgiving, Easter, or Valentine's Day card or letter instead? I have one friend who sends out the family's annual update letter on Groundhog Day. If you do this at another time of the year, you'll probably have more time and your friends and relatives will probably give it a lot more attention.

The "blessing box." Keep scrap paper near the dinner table and, a few times a month, ask family members to name something they are thankful for. Write those things down on the pieces of paper, fold them, and put them in any sort of keepsake box (cleaned-out coffee cans work just fine). Then, on Thanksgiving Day, take the scrap pieces out, read them, and recall some of the ways that God has blessed your family during the year. You might even put this "blessing box" in the center of the table as a centerpiece and offer it to God as a token of your thanksgiving and praise for the blessings of the past year.

Advent wreaths. Martin Luther is credited with popularizing the Advent wreath as a way for parents to teach children the meaning of Christmas. You can make an Advent wreath (or purchase a ready-made one at a Christian store) that is usually placed on the dining room table as a centerpiece and lighted at meals, with Scripture readings preceding the lighting of the candles. Most Advent wreaths have four purple candles in a circle and a white candle in the center; the latter is lighted on Christmas Day. There is special significance on each Sunday of Advent, as a new candle is lighted each time during the four weeks, and then the same candles are lighted each meal during the week. In this context, it provides the opportunity for family devotions and prayers together, and helps teach the story of Christ's coming to children, especially if they are involved in reading the daily Scriptures. A search on the Internet for "advent wreaths" will yield many more ideas.

Christmas tree cross. If you put up a real (as opposed to fake) Christmas tree every year, here's a great project for the handyman of the house. Rather than taking the whole tree to the recycler, cut off all the branches of the tree and save the trunk. Use the wood in the trunk to build a cross that can be displayed in your home during the Easter season. It can be a meaningful representation of how the same Jesus whose birth we celebrate on Christmas Day came to die for our sins and give us eternal life.

Family Lenten service. Whether your church observes the Lenten season (a time on the Christian calendar that runs from Ash Wednesday through Easter Sunday) or not, you might consider observing it in your home with your family. Lent is a forty-day period (not including Sundays) of fasting, penance, and prayer to commemorate the great sacrifice that Jesus made for us on the cross; it is patterned after the forty days Jesus spent fasting in the wilderness.

The common practice is for observers of Lent to fast from (or give up) something that they normally would eat, drink, or otherwise enjoy the rest of the year. Even a simple fast (like giving up soda) can serve as a daily reminder to thank Jesus for his sacrifice on the cross. It should never be legalistically done, of course, but only as a form of spiritual discipline and out of a desire to honor Christ.

If you choose to observe Lent as a family, first take the time to teach the meaning to your children (do a little research before you do so), and then decide how you want to observe Lent together. Don't just announce to your kids, "We have decided there will be no desserts for the next 40 days!"—or you may get a rebellion. Consider *doing* something you don't normally do—like saying the Lord's Prayer together at the dinner table—rather than giving up something. Any daily observance that has meaning for you will work during this special time of the year. Other suggestions:

- Choose a charity that you can give money to each day.
- Participate together in a service project each of the six weekends before Easter.
- Read special Lenten readings from the Bible each day.
- Give up something together as a family, like candy, soft drinks, meat, watching TV, video games, etc.
- Put a cross centerpiece on the dining room table and say a special prayer thanking Jesus for what he did on the cross.
- Create a "Lenten box" into which family members place something special to them each day or week (like toys or the TV remote control); again, make sure this is agreed to by all beforehand. The items then stay in the box until Easter. This can symbolize Jesus' death and resurrection.

If you want to pass a lasting faith on to your kids, you need the church—not to teach your children for you but to partner with you and support you in that effort. I probably don't need to tell you that just as there are no perfect families, so there are no perfect churches. None of them are going to be all that you need or want. But after having served in quite a few local churches in my lifetime, I'm convinced that if I were starting my family all over again, I would look for a church that had most or all of the following characteristics.

A family-friendly church. A family-friendly church is essentially a church that supports families in all of its ministries. You would think all churches supported families, but sadly, that's not the case. There are many churches these days that expect families to support the church by attending all of their services, going to all their activities, serving in all their ministries, giving to meet all their financial obligations, and bringing friends and neighbors to help make the church grow.

Churches like this provide all kinds of spiritual products and services, a bit like a religious shopping mall. Many of them are quite impressive. They are there for your convenience, with programs and ministries for virtually every age group from birth to the grave. But rather than engaging and equipping you to be the spiritual leader in your home, these churches provide programs and personnel to do it all for you. They may even have a family ministry with a counseling service and occasional parenting seminars. All you need to do is come to the church and access the appropriate program. A simple diagram would look something like this:

FAMILIES SUPPORT THE CHURCH

But family-friendly churches are different. Rather than trying to compete with families for time and resources, they recognize that the family is the primary place where faith is nurtured, strengthened, lived out, and passed on from one generation to the next. Therefore, they make sure that every ministry of the church is designed to encourage and equip parents to become spiritual leaders at home and to help the entire church become the true extended family of God.

For example, in a family-friendly church, the youth and children's ministries engage and equip parents to become the spiritual leaders in their homes.[36] The men's and women's ministries focus on strengthening families and mentoring children and youth. The senior adult ministry gives grandparents permission and encouragement to meddle in the lives of their children and grandchildren for the glory of God. The missions department of the church gets families involved in ministry together. Worship services are programmed with the whole family in mind, not just youth or baby boomers or seniors. The preaching and teaching gives parents and family members the training and tools they need to live out their faith at home. And all of the ministries of the church work together to avoid putting unnecessary pressure on family schedules. The approach looks more like this:

CHURCH SUPPORTS FAMILIES

Any church can become a family-friendly church. In fact, many churches today are becoming more family-friendly. Books like Mark Holmen's *Building Faith at Home* and Reggie Joiner's *Think Orange* have provided some much needed help and encouragement for church leaders who are ready to move their churches toward more effective ministry to parents and families.

An intergenerational church.

Again, you would think that churches would be intergenerational by nature since a church, by definition, includes all ages. But more and more churches today are anything but intergenerational. Families often arrive at the church and the parents go to worship service with adults their own age. And, of course, the senior adults have already attended a "traditional service" that took place an hour or so earlier. Meanwhile, the children are shuttled off

---

FAMILY PRAYERS

⹂ THANK YOU, SORRY, AND PLEASE PRAYERS ⹂

One way to teach young children how to pray is with some of the first words they're taught to say:

- "Thank you" (thank God for his provision)
- "Sorry" (ask God for his forgiveness)
- "Please" (ask God for his help)

Of course, this isn't just a good way for little ones to pray—it works for older folks too!

to the children's department and the teens head off to the youth group meeting located on the other side of the campus.

It really doesn't surprise me when I hear statistics about the increasing number of teenagers who leave the church when they become adults. Truth is, many of them were never part of the church when they were teenagers either. They attended a youth group that they have now outgrown. They can't relate to the church that their parents attend because there is nothing about it that is familiar to them—not the people, not the music, not the style of worship. So they either have to find a church that resembles the youth group they attended as a teenager (and quite a few of those kinds of churches are being planted these days) or they drop out of church altogether.

I know that times have changed and now we have programs for all ages, but children and youth need to be around older people, and the older people need to be around the young.

I grew up in an intergenerational church. It wasn't intergenerational by design, but by default. While there were age-segregated Sunday school classes, everything else—from the Sunday morning worship services to the once-a-month roller skating parties to the Wednesday night prayer meetings—was for everybody. When I was a youngster, I knew all the old folks in the church and they knew me. These people were incredibly important to me as spiritual mentors and examples to follow.

I know that times have changed and now we have programs for all ages, but children and youth need to be around older people, and the older people need to be around the young. It's good for both of them. For years I've told the students in my junior high group that when they become part of our youth ministry they are going to discover grandmas, grandpas, uncles, and aunts they never knew they had. That's what the church is supposed to be: the family of God. We are related to each other—brothers and sisters in Christ—and I want the young people to know that there are older people who care about them and what they do, who will be available to them for advice and mentoring, who will be praying for them. My friend Mark DeVries calls this "packing the stands" for our kids—providing them with a "mighty cloud of witnesses" (similar to the idea in Hebrews 12) who will be there cheering them on and encouraging them.

A local church. There is a growing tendency these days for people to drive long distances from their homes and neighborhoods to attend churches where the celebrity pastor preaches or the more impressive worship services are held. I realize that sometimes this cannot be avoided when a faraway church is the closest church in your particular denomination or the only one that seems to match up well with the criteria you have for a good church. But I have found that children, and teens especially, benefit from being part of a church that is close to home, where members of their faith community are also part of their geographic community. When kids know and interact with believers who attend the same schools and shop in the same stores and walk the same streets, this can provide accountability and a sense of community that can be very faith-strengthening.

A small church. Yes, size matters when it comes to churches, and contrary to the conventional wisdom, bigger is not necessarily better. I realize that's not a very popular thing to say in a day and age when so many churches want to be like the Willow Creek or Saddleback or North Point types of churches. These mega-churches are indeed impressive as they provide programs and services for tens of thousands of people every week. I've had lots of experience with churches both large and small and I can assure you that a small church can offer plenty of things that large churches simply cannot.

Let me just add that I don't believe there is any inherent virtue in smallness other than the fact that small churches generally create community a whole lot better and easier than large churches do. Churches aren't more biblical or spiritual just because they are small, nor will they automatically provide a caring community. Truth is, some churches are small simply because they have weak leadership, bad theology, and a lot of people who don't like each other very much. That's why the church has remained small and stagnant.

But large churches can have problems too, of course, and chief among them is the problem of creating community and closeness among members of the congregation. My wife and I have been part of a large church for more than fifteen years now and I'm sorry to say that I still don't know most of the congregation, even those who have been members of the church longer than we have. Fortunately, our church also has an excellent small group ministry, which has given us a way to get to know a few people on a much deeper level. But I miss being part of a small church.

I am very grateful for the small churches we attended while our children were still at home. I'll never forget overhearing a conversation that our daughter, Amber, had with one of her school friends when the subject of church came up.

"My church is so *huuuuge*!" said her friend, bragging about the mega-church she attended across town. "And our youth pastor is awesome! He plays in a cool band and knows a lot of famous people. Our youth group meets in the new gym and it's really fun! We're going to winter camp in a few weeks and later on we're going to Disneyland and Magic Mountain!"

"Well . . . " Amber said, "the people in my church love me."

A Christ-centered church. This should be obvious since it's the only thing that makes the church an actual church. You will notice that the four characteristics I've identified above could be describing almost any social club or service organization. Even the local Rotary Club could be family-friendly, intergenerational, not too big, and close to where you live. But we're not interested in socializing our children into a Christian lifestyle. What we really want is for their lives to be transformed by the power of the gospel. The church exists solely to proclaim the good news about Jesus—his death, burial, and resurrection. Regardless of the name on the front door of your church, it must be, first of all, a Christ-centered church. If a church gets that right, then there's room for improvement in every other area.

> ## ❧ TWELVE WAYS THE CHURCH CAN BLESS YOUR FAMILY ❧
>
> - Make church attendance a nonnegotiable priority for your entire family.
> - Worship *together* as a family at least once a week.
> - Take advantage of family-centered church activities like retreats and camps.
> - Get to know the adults who work with your kids at church—on a first-name basis—and let them know that you are praying for them and willing to help out in any way you can.
> - Volunteer with another parent to teach your child's Sunday school class.
> - Introduce your children to some of your adult friends at church.
> - Get involved in a small group Bible study. If you have teenagers, invite them to participate with you.
> - If you have teenagers, volunteer to help out in some way with the youth ministry—as a chaperone, small group leader, mentor, or prayer partner. (There is much more about this in my recent book, *Engaging Parents as Allies*.)
> - Invite other families from the church over to your home for dinner.
> - Encourage your children's ministry and youth ministry teams to plan activities that include parents.
> - Volunteer as a family for missions and service projects that your church sponsors.
> - Visit one of your congregation's shut-ins as a family.

youth ministry

While we're on the subject of the church, let me address the issue of youth ministry since I've been a youth worker nearly my entire adult life. And what I say here can apply to children's ministry as well.

Let me say first that youth ministry is a good thing. As a parent you might be a bit apprehensive about letting your children become involved in a ministry that seems so outrageous so much of the time. There's no denying that some of the criticism that's been aimed at youth ministry over the years has been well deserved. But youth ministry is not only a good thing, it's a God thing. I am confident that God knew what he was doing when he called the tens of thousands of men and women all over the world to come alongside our sons and daughters as youth workers and youth pastors so that they could assist us in leading them to follow Christ as adults.

One of the primary goals of youth ministry is to provide quality relationships with peers and adults who care about teenagers and share their faith and values with them.

Youth ministry is a good thing for several reasons.

First, your kids need other adults involved in their lives besides you. While you will always be the most important adult presence in your children's lives, teenagers naturally gravitate during their teen years toward other adults who will serve as mentors and role models for them. If they can't find real-life adults who will share life with them, they'll likely gravitate to celebrities and other media substitutes. It's rare for kids to find adults in their community who are comfortable with teenagers or willing to give of their time. Church youth ministries do their best to surround your kids with high-quality adults who love teenagers and are committed to their well-being.

Second, your kids need a network of friends, a community where they will be accepted and included. One of the primary goals of youth ministry is to provide quality relationships with peers and adults who care about teenagers and share their faith and values with them. The engine that drives youth ministry is relationships.

Third, your kids need a place where they will be confronted and challenged with the truth of the Word of God and learn what it means to be a follower of Jesus in today's world. Sure, they hear it from you, but they also need to hear it from other adults and peers who express it differently and in a language they can understand. I've heard this from many parents over the years: "When we tell our kids something, it goes in one ear and out the other. But when they hear it from their youth leaders—who say the same things we've been saying—our kids come home acting like they've just made the biggest discovery of their lives."

Fourth, your kids need a safe place where they can ask tough questions, share their feelings, express their doubts, challenge traditions, and decide for themselves what their values and faith will be. They can't always do these things at home or on their own. Effective youth ministries encourage and facilitate dialogue, exploration, experience, and discovery so that teenagers can get a fresh look at Jesus and make personal commitments that will last a lifetime.

Fifth, your kids need a place where they can participate in social activities that are fun without being illegal, immoral, or dangerous. Most youth workers today are experts at providing fun activities that kids enjoy and parents don't have to worry (as much) about.

I could list other benefits of this ministry but suffice it to say that the youth ministry of your church is probably not like the youth ministry you remember as a teenager. It's no longer about keeping kids busy, entertained, and off the streets. It's not all fun and games or centered around a youth-minister-as-pied-piper. Youth ministry today is about—or *should* be about—the church coming alongside and strengthening you and your family. This is an encouraging trend that has been embraced by many youth leaders from across the country.

If your church already has a youth ministry, find out how you can get involved. You will be welcomed. If it doesn't have a youth ministry, maybe you can help start one. More and more youth ministries across the country are becoming more family-based and parent-driven. This is a positive development. Just as you were never meant to parent your children alone, neither were youth workers meant to do youth ministry alone. While today's youth workers are better trained and better outfitted than ever before, they need your involvement, your support, your encouragement, and especially your prayers.

Youth pastor Jeramy Clark, in his book *After Your Drop Them Off*, writes:

. . . parents and youth workers complement one another and often provide what the other cannot. Many young people will listen to spiritual truth more readily from a discipleship-group leader than they will their mom or dad. Yet youth ministers cannot serve successfully without prayer support, encouragement, and understanding from parents. The most effective way for youth workers to reach students is through the network of students' most important relationships: their families. I see a big part of my job as fortifying families so that sons and daughters might be more receptive to the truths of Christ that are lived out in their homes.[37]

resource providers

It's tempting sometimes to think that our parents and grandparents had a great advantage over parents today in raising children in the faith. After all, the world was a lot different back then, the pace of

> **⅍ VIRTUAL SHOPPING SPREE ⅍**
>
> Visit a shopping mall with your kids and give them $100 or so of "virtual (make believe) money" to spend. Give them 30 minutes to tour the mall and decide how they would spend their money if it were real. Parents, you do this exercise too. When you finish your virtual shopping spree, grab a snack at the food court and compare your lists. Then ask, "How do you think Jesus would use all that money that we just 'spent' here?" And, "How could we use this money to help those who are less fortunate than us?" And, "What are some things we have as a family that are priceless—that don't cost any money?" This can be a good way to help your kids develop healthy attitudes toward money and material things.

life slower, the values of our culture more in line with the values of our faith. While there is some truth to all that, today's parents also have some tremendous advantages over parents of the past. As we've already noted, more and more churches—youth and children's ministries—are learning to effectively partner with parents, and today there are more resources being created and published than ever before to help parents become better equipped and more confident as the spiritual trainers of their children.

You'll have to decide what you spend your money on, but let me encourage you to take advantage of some of the great resources that are available.

Below are a few ministries I know that can provide you with some valuable help, encouragement, and a lot more good ideas. Some of these folks offer free resources, but most of them sell their products for a fee or request donations. You'll have to decide what you spend your money on, but let me encourage you to take advantage of some of the great resources that are available. By doing so you'll be making a great investment in your family.

- HomeWord (www.homeword.com) is a ministry that was founded by my good friend Jim Burns. It is now affiliated with Azusa Pacific University's Center for Youth and Family Ministries and is dedicated to helping families succeed. HomeWord offers parent seminars, a monthly parent e-newsletter, devotionals, and numerous books and publications on every aspect of parenting and family life.

- Focus on the Family (www.focusonthefamily.com) was founded by Dr. James Dobson about forty years ago and continues to be a leader in providing parents with excellent resources for raising children in the Christian faith. From its daily Focus on the Family radio broadcasts to its hundreds of books and publications for parents and church leaders, you can find help on almost any aspect of parenting and family life from this organization's deep catalog of resources.

- Vibrant Faith Ministries (www.vibrantfaith.org) for many years was known as the Youth and Family Institute, a ministry founded by legendary researcher Merton Strommen, author of *Five Cries of Parents* and many other books. For more than three decades this organization has produced a wide variety of extremely practical faith-building resources for parents and congregations.

- Family Matters (www.familymatters.net) is a nonprofit ministry founded by author and speaker Tim Kimmel. Its goal is to "see families transformed by God's grace into instruments of restoration and reformation by equipping families for every age and stage of life" (from the ministry's Web site).

- The Center for Parent/Youth Understanding (www.cpyu.org) is a ministry for parents and youth workers that was founded by a good friend, Walt Mueller. He provides valuable help for parents on how to help your kids think Christianly about popular culture. You'll find music, movie, and video game reviews, and much more.

- Al Menconi Ministries (www.almenconi.com) was founded by another friend of mine who specializes in helping young people make good entertainment choices. His Web site offers numerous resources "for parents who want to instill values in their kids."

- Family Times (www.familytimes.org) is a ministry founded by Reggie Joiner (former family ministries pastor at North Point Community Church near Atlanta, Georgia). Family Times provides parents with "easy to use tools to make the most of everyday moments together" (from the ministry's Web site).

184 generation to generation

- Mary Rice Hopkins and Company (www.maryricehopkins.com) is a ministry founded by a legend in the field of Christian children's music. Visit her Web site and you'll find lots of music, videos, and other resources that you can use to teach your children the Bible and the values of the Christian faith. Full disclosure: Mary is my sister, and yes, I'm very proud of her.

trusting god

While there are many outstanding resources available to help you in your journey as a Christian parent (and now with this book, there's one more!), I hope you'll remember that ultimately you are the one who's in the best position to know how to raise your own children. God will lead you if you are willing to trust him for the guidance and direction you need as a parent.

I'm reminded of a poem, "According to the Book," that John Maxwell quoted in one of his books:

Junior hit the meter man; Junior hit the cook.
Junior's antisocial (according to the book).
Junior smashed the clock and lamp; Junior hacked a tree.
(Destructive trends are treated in chapters 2 and 3.)

Junior threw his milk at Mom; Junior screamed for more.
(Notes on self-assertiveness are found in chapter 4.)
Junior tossed his shoes and socks out into the rain.
(Negation: that is normal; disregard the strain.)

Junior set Dad's shirt on fire; upset Grandpa's plate.
(That's to get attention—see page 38.)
Grandpa seized a slipper and turned Junior cross his knee.
(He's read nothing but the Bible since 1923.)[38]

It's a humorous attempt, of course, at saying that there aren't clinical, or even clean and easy, answers for every situation. While there's much to be gained from books by respected Christian authors, there's no substitute for the words of God himself. Of course, the Bible was never meant to be a parenting book. If you've sought scriptural guidance for raising perfect kids, you may have discovered that there's not a lot of instruction about child-rearing in the Bible.

There are many reasons for this, but perhaps the most important is that God knows that parents tend to create children in their own image—just as he did with us. We tend to pass on our values and habits to our kids, often without realizing that transfer is taking place. Therefore, God knows that if he can get us to believe and behave according to his will, we'll be more likely to pass on those beliefs and behaviors to our children. That's why the Bible doesn't spend a lot of time telling us how our children should live. It just tells us how we as parents should live.

And that has been the focus of this book. The emphasis is not on what your kids do but what you do. The only thing we have any control over is ourselves. There are absolutely no guarantees in the Bible or anywhere else that your children will follow you down the pathway of faith in Christ. You can do all that this book recommends and more and your children are still free to choose another path altogether.

I hope you'll remember that ultimately you are the one who's in the best position to know how to raise your own children. God will lead you if you are willing to trust him for the guidance and direction you need as a parent.

But what about Proverbs 22:6? Doesn't the Bible say that if we do all the right things our children will remain in the way they should go? Isn't this a promise that God has made to us?

Actually, no. The book of Proverbs is a collection of wisdom sayings that are not to be confused with the promises of God. Proverbs are principles that are true, but not absolute. Proverbs are like sayings that begin "More often than not . . ." or "In most cases . . .". While there is a high probability for a proverb to come true, exceptions are always possible.

Take, for example, Proverbs 15:1, which says, "A gentle answer turns away wrath." But what if your gentle answer is met with hostility? That doesn't make the proverb any less true. Most of the time a gentle answer *does* turn away anger, but ultimately we have no control over the responses we get from others.

The same holds true for Proverbs 22:6. While it's true that children who are taught to choose the right path will be more likely to do so than children who aren't, the Proverbs also say that it's common for children to despise their parents (15:20) and mock them (30:17). Indeed, children raised in a godly home may even be so heartless as to run through their parents' money (28:24)! Proverbs presents a very realistic view of life—not a storybook ideal.

If we follow the advice of Proverbs 22:6, there's a good probability that our children will either remain true to what they have been taught or return to it after they have matured and realize that their parents weren't so stupid after all. That, however, is only a probability. It is not a promise. If we've done our best to pass our faith and values on to our

> ### ❧ LIFE VERSES ❧
>
> Many people have "life verses" that they memorize and live their lives by. Why not take some time to sit down with your family and choose life verses for each member? Compile a list of favorite verses to choose from ahead of time, like Philippians 4:13 ("I can do everything through him who gives me strength") or Jeremiah 29:11 ("For I know the plans I have for you . . . plans to prosper you and not to harm you, plans to give you hope and a future") or Proverbs 3:5, 6 ("Trust in the Lord with all your heart and lean not on your own understanding; in all your ways acknowledge him, and he will make your paths straight"). Allow your children to choose one of these or any other that has meaning to them and then memorize the verse and make it their own personal life verse. When you get together for family worship, have each person recite his or her life verse as a reminder and as encouragement to each other.

children, then we've done all we can do. The rest is up to our kids and God. Regardless of how our kids turn out, we shouldn't take more credit than we deserve—good or bad.

I know many parents who feel a tremendous amount of guilt and shame because their children have chosen not to follow them in the footsteps of faith. Likewise, some parents love to take pride and a good deal of credit for how their trophy children turn out. But neither of these responses to how our children choose to believe or not believe is appropriate. Perhaps humility is in order here. It's natural, of course, for parents to feel deep sadness when their children reject the good news about Jesus or stray away from the values and faith that they were taught. And parents whose children have chosen to follow Christ will feel great joy and thanksgiving, which is a blessing from God. But wise parents know that there is no such thing as a perfect parent. Just as none of us deserve the great salvation that God has provided for us through his grace and mercy, so none of us deserve great outcomes in our children's lives because of how well we've done as a parent. There are no perfect parents except for God the Father himself, and he is well acquainted with our grief as well as our joy.

If we've done our best to pass our faith and values on to our children, then we've done all we can do. The rest is up to our kids and God. Regardless of how our kids turn out, we shouldn't take more credit than we deserve—good or bad.

But what we do *does* matter. I'll say it a final time: I've always believed that even though we can't do everything, we can do something. And God takes that something and blesses it and uses it in ways we can't imagine to accomplish his will in the lives of our children. Just as Jesus used a little boy's lunch to feed a multitude, so God in his great mercy uses even our feeblest efforts to woo our children to himself.

May you be one of those parents who experiences great joy and thanksgiving as you watch your children grow in faith. If you have not yet experienced that joy, may God grant you patience as you wait. Remember that God isn't finished with our kids, no matter how old they are. He's not finished with any of us.

QUESTIONS FOR REFLECTION AND ACTION

1 ‖ How has your local church provided support for you and your family?

2 ‖ Who are the people in your church or community who are having a positive influence on your children? The most positive impact on their faith? How can you see to it that your kids spend more time with them?

3 ‖ How could you become a mentor to somebody else's children? In what ways can you do this while being responsible with your time and keeping your kids first?

4 || To whom do you turn when you are struggling as a parent?

5 || How can you enlist others to pray for you and your family? List a few prayer requests below and then share them with people in your family or church who will commit to joining you in prayer.

INDEX OF ACTIVITIES AND IDEAS

You may find a number of these working in more than one category, as a few have been designated below.

Faith Conversation Starters

Family Devotions

Family Dinner Discussion Ideas

Family Fun

Family Prayer Ideas

Family Service Projects

Family Traditions

Family Vacations

Holiday Celebrations

Easter

Thanksgiving

Christmas

More Holiday Activities

Tools for Parents

Parenting Self-Assessment

Setting Goals

Special Family Services

ABOUT WAYNE RICE

 Wayne Rice is a veteran youth worker, author, speaker, and ministry consultant. He cofounded Youth Specialties, a non-denominational organization that has provided resources and training for youth workers for more than four decades. He is also the founder of Understanding Your Teenager, a ministry that serves parents of teens and pre-teens, which is now part of HomeWord (www.homeword.com). He frequently conducts seminars for parents of children of all ages and speaks at conferences and training events for parents, youth workers, and Christian leaders. He currently serves as family ministries coach at College Avenue Baptist Church in San Diego.

Wayne is the author of more than thirty books for parents and youth workers, including *Read This Book or You're Grounded, There's a Teenager in My House,* and *Engaging Parents as Allies.* Many of his books have become youth ministry best sellers.

Wayne's hobby is bluegrass music. He has played banjo and guitar in several bands and has hosted a bluegrass music radio show in San Diego for almost thirty-five years. Visit his Web site (www.waynerice.com) and you can watch a video of Wayne playing and singing with Johnny Cash.

Wayne and his wife, Marci, have been married since 1966 and live in Lakeside, California. They have three grown children and, so far, three grandchildren.

NOTES

1. "LifeWay Research Uncovers Reasons 18 to 22 Year Olds Drop Out of Church," LifeWay staff, www.lifeway.com/lwc/article_main_page/ 0%2C1703%2CA%25253D165949%252526M%25253D200906 %2C00.html? (accessed January 3, 2010).

2. Christian Smith with Melinda Lundquist Denton, *Soul Searching: The Religious and Spiritual Lives of American Teenagers* (New York: Oxford University Press, 2005), 261.

3. Reggie Joiner, *Think Orange: Imagine the Impact When Church and Family Collide* (Colorado Springs: David C. Cook, 2009), 86-89.

4. A 2007 study conducted by the Associated Press and MTV found that nearly three-quarters of America's teens say they are happiest when they are with their parents. http://news.yahoo.com/s/ap/20070819/ ap_on_re_us/youth_poll_happiness (accessed January 3, 2010).

5. Romans 5:12-21; 1 Corinthians 15:22; 1 Thessalonians 1:9.

6. Genesis 27:28, 29; Genesis 48, 49.

7. Wayne Rice, *Enjoy Your Middle Schooler: A Guide to Understanding the Physical, Social, Emotional and Spiritual Challenges of Your 11-14 Year Old* (Grand Rapids: Zondervan, 1994), 16.

8. "Stereotypes Can Fuel Teen Misbehavior," Reuters, October 16, 2009, www.reuters.com/article/pressRelease/idUS168645+16-Oct-2009+PRN20091016?sp=true (accessed December 8, 2009).

9. Adapted from Mark Holmen's *Faith Begins at Home: The Family Makeover with Christ at the Center* (Ventura, Calif.: Regal Books, 2005), 28-34.

10. U.S. Department of Labor, Bureau of Labor Statistics Economic News Release, "Time spent caring for household children under 18 by sex of adult and age of youngest child by day of week, average for the combined years 2004-08," http://www.bls.gov/news.release/atus.t09.htm (accessed December 11, 2009).

11. Jim Burns, *How to Be a Happy, Healthy Family: Ten Principles of Families That Succeed* (Nashville, Tenn.: Thomas Nelson, 2001), 84.

12. Ibid., 2.

13. M. Scott Peck, *The Road Less Traveled: A New Psychology of Love, Traditional Values and Spiritual Growth* (New York: Simon & Schuster, 1978), 121-123.

14. David Elkind, *All Grown Up and No Place to Go* (Reading, Mass.: Addison-Wesley, 1984), 204.

15. Matea Gold, *The L.A. Times,* "Kids watch more than a day of TV each week," October 27, 2009, http://articles.latimes.com/2009/oct/27/entertainment/et-kids-tv27 (accessed January 7, 2010).

16. Smith with Denton, *Soul Searching,* 262, 270.

17. Ibid., 162, 163.

18. Ibid., 164.

19. See many examples of the "Creeds of Christendom" at www.creeds.net/.

20. Joseph L. Mangina, *Karl Barth: Theologian of Christian Witness* (Louisville, Ky.: Westminster John Knox Press, 2004), 9.

21. Stephen Covey, A. Roger Merrill, and Rebecca R. Merrill, *First Things First* (New York: Simon & Schuster, 1994), 51.

22. Tony Campolo, *Red Letter Christians: A Citizen's Guide to Faith and Politics* (Ventura, Calif.: Regal Books, 2008).

23. In fact, the book *The Jesus Creed: Loving God, Loving Others*, by Scot McKnight (Paraclete Press, 2004), takes more than three hundred pages to unpack the theology associated with just the four words that comprise the book's subtitle.

24. Marlene LeFever, *Learning Styles: Reaching Everyone God Gave You* (Colorado Springs: David C. Cook, 1995), 19-21.

25. Anthony T. Evans, *Guiding Your Family in a Misguided World* (Pomona, Calif.: Focus on the Family, 1991), 54.

26. Bill McNabb and Steven Mabry, *Teaching the Bible Creatively: How to Awaken Your Kids to Scripture* (Grand Rapids: Zondervan, 1990), 42.

27. John H. Westerhoff III described this in his book *Will Our Children Have Faith?* (Morehouse Publishing, 1976). See also James W. Fowler, *Stages of Faith: The Psychology of Human Development and the Quest for Meaning* (HarperOne, 1995).

28. Tim Stafford, *Never Mind the Joneses: Building Core Christian Values in a Way That Fits Your Family* (Downers Grove, Ill.: InterVarsity Press, 2004), 19, 20.

29. David Elkind, *Ties That Stress: The New Family Imbalance* (Cambridge, Mass.: Harvard University Press, 1994), 57.

30. "Teens in households where dinners are infrequent and such distractions [such as cell phones, texting, watching TV] are present at the table are three times likelier to use marijuana and tobacco; and two a half times likelier to use alcohol." The quote is from the study "The Importance of Family Dinners V," September 2009, by the National Center on Addiction and Substance Abuse at Columbia University.

31. M. Scott Peck, *The Different Drum: Community Making and Peace* (New York: Simon & Schuster, 1987), 25.

32. From "Effective Christian Education: A National Study of Protestant Congregations," conducted by Search Institute in 1990. The results of this study were reprinted in Mark Holmen, *Building Faith at Home: Why Faith at Home Must Be Your Church's #1 Priority* (Ventura, Calif.: Regal Books, 2007), 26.

33. Jay Kesler, *Grand Parenting: The Agony and the Ecstasy* (Ann Arbor, Mich.: Servant Publications, 1993), 18.

34. "New Research Explores the Long-Term Effect of Spiritual Activity among Children and Teens," Barna Research, November 16, 2009, www.barna.org/barna-update/article/15-familykids/321-new-research-explores-the-long-term-effect-of-spiritual-activity-among-children-and-teens (accessed November 16, 2009).

35. Kevin DeYoung and Ted Kluck, *The Washington Post*, "Church: Love It, Don't Leave It," in The Washington Post online, July 1, 2009, http://newsweek.washingtonpost.com/onfaith/guestvoices/2009/07/church_love_it_dont_leave_it.html (accessed December 23, 2009).

36. I've written a book for youth leaders, by the way, called *Engaging Parents as Allies*, from the Youth Ministry In the Trenches series (Cincinnati: Standard Publishing, 2009).

37. Jeramy and Jerusha Ann Clark, *After You Drop Them Off: A Parent's Guide to Student Ministry* (Colorado Springs: Waterbrook Press, 2005), 4.

38. John C. Maxwell, *Breakthrough Parenting* (Colorado Springs: Focus on the Family, 1996), 81.